Junior Great Books

4

BOOK ONE

CAPE PTSO #2

Junior Great Books®

Trust
Resourcefulness
Communication

BOOK ONE

The Great Books Foundation

A nonprofit educational organization

Copyright © 2014 by The Great Books Foundation

Chicago, Illinois

ISBN 978-1-939014-51-1

2 4 6 8 9 7 5 3 1

Printed in the United States of America

Published and distributed by

THE GREAT BOOKS FOUNDATION
A nonprofit educational organization

35 East Wacker Drive, Suite 400

Chicago, IL 60601

www.greatbooks.org

CONTENTS

Resourcefulness

Communication

INTRODUCTION

Welcome to Junior Great Books! In this program, you will be reading stories and discussing your ideas about them. Before you begin, here are some important things to know.

The stories in Junior Great Books will make you wonder about things. You might wonder what a word means, why the author told the story this way, or why a character does something. That's because authors do not usually tell us exactly how the parts of a story are connected or explain why everything in a story happens.

But in good writing, everything fits together and is there for a reason, even if it is not completely explained for you. Good authors put into their writing the things a reader must know to understand what is happening and why. As a good reader, you need to look closely at the writing to discover these things. In Junior Great Books, you will use a learning process called **Shared Inquiry**™ to help you do that.

How Shared Inquiry Works

In Shared Inquiry, you read stories that make you think and ask questions.

Usually you will begin work on a story by reading along as you hear the story read aloud. After everyone has read the story, the group shares questions about it. Any question you have about the story is worth asking. Some questions can be answered right away. Others will be saved for the discussion or other activities.

Next, everyone reads the story again. During the second reading you will do some activities that will help you understand the story better. These activities may include taking notes, sharing your thoughts about the story with a partner, or acting out scenes from the story.

You will then develop your ideas about the story even more in **Shared Inquiry discussion.**

What Shared Inquiry Discussion Looks Like

In your discussion, you will sit so that everyone can see and hear one another. Your teacher will start the discussion with an **interpretive question**—a question that has more than one good answer that can be supported with evidence from the story. So in Shared Inquiry discussion, the teacher isn't looking for the "right answer" to the question, but is interested in hearing different ideas about it.

During the discussion, the teacher asks more questions that help everyone think deeply and explain their ideas.

Besides sharing your ideas, you can agree or disagree with a classmate or ask someone a question about a comment. You can also ask someone to explain an idea.

At the end of the discussion, people will have different answers to the interpretive question. But everyone will have evidence for his or her answer and a better understanding of the story. You may change your answer because of what you hear in the discussion, or you may hear new evidence to support your original answer.

After the discussion, you may do other activities based on the story. You may write about your answer to the discussion question or do a creative writing activity. Or you may make artwork, compose a song, or do research about something in the story.

I've been thinking about what you said . . .

You may find that even after the class has finished working on a story, you are still thinking about it. The characters and events in a story may help you think about your own life and the people around you in new ways, or suggest a new subject you are interested in.

Every time you ask a question about a story or discuss an interpretive question with your classmates, you are increasing your skills as a reader and thinker. You are also learning how stories work and what kinds of stories you enjoy. You are becoming a better reader.

Dos and Don'ts in Discussion

DO

Let other people talk, and listen to what they say.

DON'T

Talk while other people are talking.

DO

Share your ideas about the story. You may have an idea no one else has thought of.

DON'T

Be afraid to say what you're thinking about the story.

DO

Be polite when
you disagree with
someone.

DON'T

Get angry when
someone disagrees
with you.

DO

Pay attention to
the person who
is talking.

DON'T

Do things that make
it hard for people
to pay attention.

Shared Inquiry Discussion Guidelines

Following these guidelines in Shared Inquiry discussion will help everyone share ideas about the story and learn from one another.

1 Listen to or read the story twice before the discussion.

2 Discuss only the story that everyone has read.

3 Support your ideas with evidence from the story.

4 Listen to other people's ideas. You may agree or disagree with someone's answer, or ask a question about it.

5 Expect the teacher to only ask questions.

Theme Introduction

Trust

In this section of the book, you will read about characters who want to trust each other, or who are afraid to trust each other. Thinking about these stories, and about your own experiences with trust, will give you new ideas about what it means to trust other people and be trusted by them.

IMPORTANT QUESTIONS TO THINK ABOUT

Before starting this section, think about your own experiences with trust:

- Who do you trust the most?

- How do you feel when you know someone trusts you?

- How does it feel when you know you can trust someone?

Once you have thought about your own experiences with trust, think about this **theme question** and write down your answers or share them aloud:

How do you earn someone's trust?

After reading each story in this section, ask yourself the theme question again. You may have some new ideas you want to add.

It was about eleven o'clock at night.

THANK YOU, M'AM

Langston Hughes

She was a large woman with a large purse that had everything in it but a hammer and nails. It had a long strap, and she carried it slung across her shoulder. It was about eleven o'clock at night, dark, and she was walking alone, when a boy ran up behind her and tried to snatch her purse. The strap broke with the sudden single tug the boy gave it from behind. But the boy's weight and the weight of the purse combined caused him to lose his balance. Instead of taking off full blast as he had hoped, the boy fell on his back on the sidewalk and his legs flew up. The large woman simply turned around and kicked him right square in his blue-jeaned sitter. Then she reached down, picked the boy up by his shirt front, and shook him until his teeth rattled.

After that the woman said, "Pick up my pocketbook, boy, and give it here."

She still held him tightly. But she bent down enough to permit him to stoop and pick up her purse. Then she said, "Now ain't you ashamed of yourself?"

Firmly gripped by his shirt front, the boy said, "Yes'm."

The woman said, "What did you want to do it for?"

The boy said, "I didn't aim to."

She said, "You a lie!"

By that time two or three people passed, stopped, turned to look, and some stood watching.

"If I turn you loose, will you run?" asked the woman.

"Yes'm," said the boy.

"Then I won't turn you loose," said the woman. She did not release him.

"Lady, I'm sorry," whispered the boy.

"Um-hum! Your face is dirty. I got a great mind to wash your face for you. Ain't you got nobody home to tell you to wash your face?"

"No'm," said the boy.

"Then it will get washed this evening," said the large woman, starting up the street, dragging the frightened boy behind her.

He looked as if he were fourteen or fifteen, frail and willow-wild, in tennis shoes and blue jeans.

The woman said, "You ought to be my son. I would teach you right from wrong. Least I can do right now is to wash your face. Are you hungry?"

"No'm," said the being-dragged boy. "I just want you to turn me loose."

"Was I bothering *you* when I turned that corner?" asked the woman.

"No'm."

"But you put yourself in contact with *me*," said the woman. "If you think that that contact is not going to last awhile, you got another thought coming. When I get through with you, sir, you are going to remember Mrs. Luella Bates Washington Jones."

Sweat popped out on the boy's face and he began to struggle. Mrs. Jones stopped, jerked him around in front of her, put a half nelson about his neck, and continued to drag him up the street. When she got to her door, she dragged the boy inside, down a hall, and into a large kitchenette-furnished room at the rear of the house. She switched on the light and left the door open. The boy could hear other roomers laughing and talking in the large house. Some of their doors were open, too, so he knew he and the woman were not alone. The woman still had him by the neck in the middle of her room.

She said, "What is your name?"

"Roger," answered the boy.

"Then, Roger, you go to that sink and wash your face," said the woman, whereupon she turned him loose—at last. Roger looked at the door—looked at the woman—looked at the door—*and went to the sink.*

"Let the water run until it gets warm," she said. "Here's a clean towel."

"You gonna take me to jail?" asked the boy, bending over the sink.

"Not with that face, I would not take you nowhere," said the woman. "Here I am trying to get home to cook me a bite to eat, and you snatch my pocketbook! Maybe you ain't been to your supper either, late as it be. Have you?"

"There's nobody home at my house," said the boy.

16

"Then we'll eat," said the woman. "I believe you're hungry—or been hungry—to try to snatch my pocketbook!"

"I want a pair of blue suede shoes," said the boy.

"Well, you didn't have to snatch *my* pocketbook to get some suede shoes," said Mrs. Luella Bates Washington Jones. "You could of asked me."

"M'am?"

The water dripping from his face, the boy looked at her. There was a long pause. A very long pause. After he had dried his face and not knowing what else to do, dried it again, the boy turned around, wondering what next. The door was open. He could make a dash for it down the hall. He could run, run, run, *run*!

The woman was sitting on the daybed. After a while she said, "I were young once and I wanted things I could not get."

There was another long pause. The boy's mouth opened. Then he frowned, not knowing he frowned.

The woman said, "Um-hum! You thought I was going to say *but*, didn't you? You thought I was going to say, *but I didn't snatch people's pocketbooks.* Well, I wasn't going to say that." Pause. Silence. "I have done things, too, which I would not tell you, son—neither tell God, if he didn't already know. Everybody's got something in common. So you set down while I fix us something to eat. You might run that comb through your hair so you will look presentable."

In another corner of the room behind a screen was a gas plate and an icebox. Mrs. Jones got up and went behind the screen. The woman did not watch the boy to see if he was going to run now, nor did she watch her purse, which she left behind her on the daybed. But the boy took care to sit on the far side of the room, away from the purse, where he thought she could easily see him out of the corner of her eye if she wanted to. He did not trust the woman *not* to trust him. And he did not want to be mistrusted now.

"Do you need somebody to go to the store," asked the boy, "maybe to get some milk or something?"

"Don't believe I do," said the woman, "unless you just want sweet milk yourself. I was going to make cocoa out of this canned milk I got here."

"That will be fine," said the boy.

She heated some lima beans and ham she had in the icebox, made the cocoa, and set the table. The woman did not ask the boy anything about where he lived, or his folks, or anything else that would embarrass him. Instead, as they ate, she told him about her job in a hotel beauty shop that stayed

open late, what the work was like, and how all
kinds of women came in and out, blondes, redheads,
and Spanish. Then she cut him a half of her
ten-cent cake.

"Eat some more, son," she said.

When they were finished eating, she got up
and said, "Now here, take this ten dollars and buy
yourself some blue suede shoes. And next time,
do not make the mistake of latching onto *my*
pocketbook *nor nobody else's*—because shoes got by
devilish ways will burn your feet. I got to get my rest
now. But from here on in, son, I hope you will behave
yourself."

She led him down the hall to the front door
and opened it. "Good night! Behave yourself,
boy!" she said, looking out into the street
as he went down the steps.

The boy wanted to say something other than, "Thank you, m'am," to Mrs. Luella Bates Washington Jones, but although his lips moved, he couldn't even say that as he turned at the foot of the barren stoop and looked up at the large woman in the door. Then she shut the door.

Tentatively I call again, more loudly.

CROW CALL

Lois Lowry

It's morning, early, barely light, cold for November. At home, in the bed next to mine, Jessica, my older sister, still sleeps. But my bed is empty.

I sit shyly in the front seat of the car next to the stranger who is my father, my legs pulled up under the too-large wool shirt I am wearing.

I practice his name to myself, whispering it under my breath. *Daddy. Daddy.* Saying it feels new. The war has lasted so long. He has been gone so long. Finally I look over at him timidly and speak aloud.

"Daddy," I say, "I've never gone hunting before. What if I don't know what to do?"

"Well, Liz," he says, "I've been thinking about that, and I've decided to put you in charge of the crow call. Have you ever operated a crow call?"

I shake my head. "No."

"It's an art," he says. "No doubt about that. But I'm pretty sure you can handle it. Some people will blow and blow on a crow call and not a single crow will even wake up or bother to listen, much less answer. But I really think you can do it. Of course," he adds, chuckling, "having that shirt will help."

My father had bought the shirt for me. In town to buy groceries, he had noticed my hesitating in front of Kronenberg's window. The plaid hunting shirts had been in the store window for a month—the popular red-and-black and green-and-black ones toward the front, clothing mannequins holding duck decoys; but my shirt, the rainbow plaid, hung separately on a wooden hanger toward the back of the display. I had lingered in front of Kronenberg's window every chance I had since the hunting shirts had appeared.

My sister had rolled her eyes in disdain. "Daddy," she pointed out to him as we entered Kronenberg's, "that's a *man's* shirt."

The salesman had smiled and said dubiously, "I don't quite think . . ."

"You know, Lizzie," my father had said to me as the salesman wrapped the shirt, "buying this shirt is probably a very practical thing to do. You will never *ever* outgrow this shirt."

Now, as we go into a diner for breakfast, the shirt unfolds itself downward until the bottom of it reaches my knees; from the bulky thickness of rolled-back cuffs, my hands are exposed. I feel totally surrounded by shirt.

My father orders coffee for himself. The waitress asks, "What about your boy? What does he want?"

My father winks at me, and I hope that my pigtails will stay hidden inside the plaid wool collar. Holding my head very still, I look at the menu. At home my usual breakfast is cereal with honey and milk. My mother keeps honey in a covered silver pitcher. There's no honey on the diner's menu.

"What's your favorite thing to eat in the whole world?" asks my father.

I smile at him. "Cherry pie," I admit. If he hadn't been away for so long, he would have known. My mother had even put birthday candles on a cherry pie on my last birthday. It was a family joke in a family that hadn't included Daddy.

My father hands back both menus to the waitress. "Three pieces of cherry pie," he tells her.

"Three?" She looks at him sleepily, not writing the order down. "You mean two?"

"No," he said, "I mean three. One for me, with black coffee, and two for my hunting companion, with a large glass of milk."

She shrugs.

We eat quickly, watching the sun rise across the Pennsylvania farmlands. Back in the car, I flip my pigtails out from under my shirt collar and giggle.

"Hey, boy," my father says to me in an imitation of the groggy waitress's voice, "you sure you can eat all that cherry pie, boy?"

"Just you watch me, lady," I answer in a deep voice, pulling my face into stern, serious lines. We laugh again, driving out into the gray-green hills of the early morning.

It's not far to the place he has chosen, not long until he pulls the car to the side of the empty road and stops.

Grass, frozen after its summer softness, crunches under our feet; the air is sharp and supremely clear, free from the floating pollens of summer, and our words seem etched and breakable on the brittle stillness. I feel the smooth wood of the crow call in my pocket, moving my fingers against it for warmth,

memorizing its ridges and shape. I stamp my feet
hard against the ground now and then as my father
does. I want to scamper ahead of him like a puppy,
kicking the dead leaves and reaching the unknown
places first, but there is an uneasy feeling along the
edge of my back at the thought of walking in front
of someone who is a *hunter*. The word makes me
uneasy. Carefully I stay by his side.

It is quieter than summer. There are no animal
sounds, no bird-waking noises; even the occasional
leaf that falls within our vision does so in silence,
spiraling slowly down to blend in with the others.

But most leaves are already gone from the trees; those that remain catch there by accident, waiting for the wind that will free them. Our breath is steam.

"Daddy," I ask shyly, "were you scared in the war?"

He looks ahead, up the hill, and after a moment he says, "Yes. I was scared."

"Of what?"

"Lots of things. Of being alone. Of being hurt. Of hurting someone else."

"Are you still?"

He glances down. "I don't think so. Those kinds of scares go away."

"I'm scared sometimes," I confide.

He nods, unsurprised. "I know," he said. "Are you scared now?"

I start to say no. Then I remember the word that scares me. *Hunter.*

I answer, "Maybe a little."

I look at his gun, his polished, waxed prize, and then at him. He nods, not saying anything. We walk on.

"Daddy?"

"Mmmmmm?" He is watching the sky, the trees.

"I wish the crows didn't eat the crops."

"They don't know any better," he says. "Even people do bad things without meaning to."

"Yes, but . . ." I pause and then say what I'd been thinking. "They might have babies to take care of. Baby crows."

"Not now, Liz, not this time of year," he says. "By now their babies are grown. It's a strange thing, but by now they don't even know who their babies are." He puts his free arm over my shoulders for a moment.

"And their babies grow up and eat the crops, too," I say, and sigh, knowing it to be true and unchangeable.

"It's too bad," he says. We begin to climb the hill.

"Can you call anything else, Daddy? Or just crows?"

"Sure," he says. "Listen. *Mooooooooo.* That's a cow call."

"Guess the cows didn't hear it," I tease.

"Well, of course, sometimes they choose not to answer. I can do tigers, too. *Rrrrrrrrrr.*"

"Ha. So can I. And bears. Better watch out, now. Bears might come out of the woods on this one. *Grrrrrrrrr.*"

"You think you're so smart, doing bears. Listen to this. Giraffe call." He stands with his neck stretched out, soundless.

I try not to laugh, wanting to do rabbits next, but I can't keep from it. He looks so funny, with his neck pulled away from his shirt collar and a condescending, poised, giraffe look on his face. I giggle at him and we keep walking to the top of the hill.

From where we stand, we can see almost back to town. We can look down on our car and follow the ribbon of road through the farmlands until it is lost in trees. Dark roofs of houses lay scattered, separated by pastures.

"Okay, Lizzie," says my father, "this is a good place. You can do the crow call now."

I see no crows. For a moment, the fear of disappointing him struggles with my desire to blow into the smooth, polished tip of the crow call. But I

see that he's waiting, and I take it from my pocket,
hold it against my lips, and blow softly.

The harsh, muted sound of a sleepy crow comes
as a surprise to me, and I smile at it, at the delight of
having made that sound myself. I do it again, softly.

From a grove of trees on another hill comes an
answer from a waking bird. Just one, and then
silence.

Tentatively I call again, more loudly. The branches
of a nearby tree rustle, and crows answer, fluttering
and calling crossly. They fly briefly into the air and
then settle on a branch—three of them.

"Look, Daddy," I whisper. "Do you see them? They think *I'm* a crow!"

He nods, watching them.

I move away from him and stand on a rock at the top of the hill and blow loudly several times. Crows rise from all the trees. They scream with harsh voices and I respond, blowing again and again as they fly from the hillside in circles, dipping and soaring, landing speculatively, lurching from the limbs in afterthought and then settling again with resolute and disgruntled shrieks.

"Listen, Daddy! Do you hear them? They think I'm their friend! Maybe their baby, all grown up!"

I run about the top of the hill and then down, through the frozen grass, blowing the crow call over and over. The crows call back at me, and from all the trees they rise, from all the hills. They circle and circle, and the morning is filled with the patterns of calling crows as I look back, still running. I can see my father sitting on a rock, and I can see he is smiling.

My crow calling comes in shorter and shorter spurts as I become breathless; finally I stop and stand laughing at the foot of the hill, and the noise from the crows subsides as they circle and settle back in the trees. They are waiting for me.

My father comes down the hill to meet me coming up. He carries his gun carefully; and though I am grateful to him for not using it, I feel that there is no need to say thank you—Daddy knows this already. The crows will always be there and they will always eat the crops; and some other morning, on some other hill, a hunter, maybe not my daddy, will take aim.

I blow the crow call once more, to say good morning and goodbye and everything that goes in between. Then I put it into the pocket of my shirt and reach over, out of my enormous cuff, and take my father's hand.

"Not now," Dan said quietly. *"Later."*

FRESH

Philippa Pearce

The force of water through the river gates scoured to a deep bottom; then the river shallowed again. People said the pool below the gates was very deep. Deep enough to drown in anyway.

At the bottom of the pool lived the freshwater mussels. No one had seen them there—most people would not have been particularly interested in them anyway. But if you were poking about among the stones in the shallows below the pool, you couldn't help finding mussel shells occasionally. Sometimes one by itself; sometimes two still hinged together. Grey-blue or green-grey on the outside; on the inside, a faint sheen of mother-of-pearl.

The Webster boys were fishing with their nets in the shallows for minnows, freshwater shrimps—

anything that moved—when they found a freshwater mussel that was not just a pair of empty shells.

Dan Webster found it. He said, "Do you want this shell? It's double." While Laurie Webster was saying, "Let's see," Dan was lifting it and had noticed that the two shells were clamped together and that they had unusual weight. "They're not empty shells," he said. "They've something inside. It's alive."

He stooped again to hold the mussel in the palm of his hand so that the river water washed over it. Water creatures prefer water.

Laurie had splashed over to him. Now he crouched with the river lapping near the tops of his Wellington boots. "A freshwater mussel!" he said. "I've never owned one." He put out fingers to touch it—perhaps to take it—as it lay on the watery palm of Dan's hand. Dan's fingers curled up into a protective wall. "Careful," he said.

Together, as they were now, the Webster boys looked like brothers, but they were cousins. Laurie was the visitor. He lived in London and had an aquarium on his bedroom windowsill, instead of a river almost at his back door as Dan had. Dan was older than Laurie; Laurie admired Dan, and Dan was kind to Laurie. They did things together. Dan helped Laurie to find livestock for his aquarium—shrimps, leeches, flatworms, water snails variously whorled; whatever the turned stone and stooping net might bring them. During a visit by Laurie, they would fish often, but—until the last day—without a jam jar, just for the fun of it. On the last day, they took a jam jar and put their more interesting catches into it for Laurie's journey back to London.

Now they had found a freshwater mussel on the second day of Laurie's visit. Five more days still to go.

"We can't keep it," said Dan. "Even if we got the jam jar, it couldn't live in a jam jar for five days. It would be dead by the time you got it back to the aquarium."

Laurie, who was quite young, looked as if he might cry. "I've never had the chance of a freshwater mussel before."

"Well . . ." said Dan. He made as if to put it down among the stones and mud where he had found it.

"Don't! Don't! It's my freshwater mussel! Don't let it go!"

"And don't shout in my ear!" Dan said crossly. "Who said I was letting it go? I was just trying it out in the river again, to see whether it was safe to leave it there. I don't think the current would carry it away."

37

He put the mussel down in the shelter of a large, slimy stone. The current, breaking on the stone, flowed past without stirring it. But the mussel began to feel at home again. They could almost see it settling contentedly into the mud. After a while it parted the lips of its shells slightly, and a pastry-like substance crowded out a little way.

"What's it *doing*?" whispered Laurie. But this was not the sort of thing that Dan knew, and Laurie would not find out until he got back to his aquarium books in London.

Now they saw that they had not merely imagined the mussel to be settling in. There was less of it visible out of the mud—much less of it.

"It's burying itself. It's escaping," said Laurie. "Don't let it!"

Dan sighed and took the mussel back into the palm of his hand again. The mussel, disappointed, shut up tight.

"We need to keep it in the river," said Dan, "but somewhere where it can't escape."

They looked around. They weren't sure what they were looking for, and at first they certainly weren't finding it.

Still with the mussel in his hand, Dan turned to the banks. They were overhanging, with river water swirling against them and under them. The roots of trees and bushes made a kind of very irregular lattice fencing through which the water ran continually.

"I wonder . . ." said Dan.

"You couldn't keep it there," Laurie said. "It'd be child's play for a freshwater mussel to escape through the roots."

Dan stared at the roots. "I've a better idea," he said. "I'll stay here with the mussel. You go back to our house—to the larder. You'll find a little white plastic carton with Eileen's slimming cress growing in it." Eileen was Dan's elder sister, whose absorbing interest was her figure. "Empty the cress out onto a plate—I'll square Eileen later. Bring the plastic carton back here."

Laurie never questioned Dan. He set off across the meadows towards the house.

Dan and the freshwater mussel were left alone to wait.

Dan was holding the freshwater mussel as he had done before, stooping down to the river with his hand in the water. It occurred to him to repeat the experiment that Laurie had interrupted. He put the mussel down in the lee of the slimy stone again and watched. Again the current left the mussel undisturbed. Again the mussel began to settle itself into the mud between the stones.

Down—gently down—down. . . . The freshwater mussel was now as deep in the mud as when Laurie had called out in fear of losing it; but now Laurie was not there. Dan did not interfere. He simply watched the mussel ease itself down—down. . . .

Soon less than a quarter of an inch of mussel shell was showing above the mud. The shell was nearly the same colour as the mud embedding it: Dan could identify it only by keeping his eyes fixed continuously upon its projection. That lessened, until it had almost disappeared.

Entirely disappeared. . . .

Still Dan stared. As long as he kept his eyes on the spot where the mussel had disappeared, he could get it again. He had only to dig his fingers into the mud at that exact spot to find it. If he let his eyes stray, the mussel was lost forever; there were so many slimy

stones like that one, and mud was everywhere. He
must keep his eyes fixed on the spot.

"Dan—Dan—Dan!" Laurie's voice came over the
meadows. "I've got it!"

He nearly shifted his stare from the spot by the
nondescript stone. It would have been so natural to
lift his head in response to the calling voice. He was
tempted to do it. But he had to remember that this
was Laurie's mussel, and it must not be lost; he did
remember. He kept his gaze fixed and dug
quickly with his fingers and got the
mussel again.

There he was standing with
the mussel in the palm of his
hand, and water and mud
dripping from it, when Laurie
came in sight. "Is it all right?"
he shouted.

"Yes," said Dan.

Laurie climbed down the
riverbank into the water with the
plastic carton in his hand. Dan
looked at it and nodded. "It has
holes in the bottom, and we can
make some more along the sides
with a penknife." He did so,
while Laurie held the mussel.

41

"Now," Dan said, "put the mussel in the
carton with some mud and little stones to make
it comfortable. That's it. The next thing is to
wedge the carton between the roots under the
bank at just the right level, so that the water flows
through the holes in the carton, without flowing
over the whole thing. The mussel will have his
flowing river, but he won't be able to escape."

Laurie said, "I wish I could think of things
like that."

Dan tried fitting the plastic carton between the
roots in several different places, until he found a grip
that was just at the right height. Gently he tested the
firmness of the wedging, and it held.

"Oh," said Laurie, "it's just perfect, Dan. Thank
you. I shall really get it back to the aquarium now.
My first freshwater mussel. I shall call it—well, what
would *you* call it, Dan?" "Go on," said Dan. "It's your
freshwater mussel. You name it."

"I shall call it Fresh then." Laurie leaned forward
to see Fresh, already part buried in his mud, dim
in the shadow of the bank, but absolutely a captive.
He stood up again and moved back to admire the
arrangement from a distance. Then he realized a
weakness. "Oh, it'll never do. The plastic's so white.
Anyone might notice it and come over to look, and
tip Fresh out."

"We'll hide him then," said Dan. He found an old brick among the stones of the shallows and brought it over to the bank roots. He upended the brick in the water, leaning it in a casual pose against the roots, so that it concealed the white plastic carton altogether.

"There," he said.

Laurie sighed. "Really perfect."

"He should be safe there."

"For five days?"

"I tell you what," said Dan, "we could slip down here every day just to have a check on him. To make sure the level of the water through the carton isn't too high or hasn't sunk too low."

Laurie nodded. "Every day."

The daily visit to Fresh was a pleasure that Laurie looked forward to. On the third day it poured with rain, but they put on anoraks as well as boots and made their check as usual. On the fourth day, they reached the riverbank to find a man fishing on the other side of the pool.

The fisherman was minding his own business and only gave them a sidelong glance as they came to a stop on the bank above Fresh's watery dungeon. (They knew its location exactly by now, even from across the meadow.) The man wasn't interested in them—yet. But if they clambered down into the river and began moving old bricks and poking about behind them, he would take notice. He would ask them what they were up to. When they had gone, he would perhaps come over and have a look for himself. He was wearing waders.

"Not now," Dan said quietly. "Later." And they turned away, as though they had come only to look at the view.

They went back after their tea, but the fisherman was

still there. In the meantime, Laurie had worked himself into a desperation. "All that rain yesterday has made the river rise. It'll be washing Fresh out of the carton."

"No," said Dan. "You've just got Fresh on the brain. The river's hardly risen at all. If at all. Fresh is all right."

"Why can't that man go home?"

"He'll go home at dusk anyway," said Dan.

"That'll be too late for us. I shall be going to bed by then. You know your mum said I must."

"Yes." Dan looked at him thoughtfully. "Would you like *me* to come? I mean, Mum couldn't stop my being out that bit later than you, because I am that bit older."

"Oh, would you—*would* you?" cried Laurie. "Oh, thanks, Dan."

"Oh, don't thank me," said Dan.

Everything went according to plan, except that Dan, getting down to the river just before dark, found the fisherman still there. But he was in the act of packing up. He did not see Dan. He packed up and walked away, whistling sadly to himself. When the whistling had died away, Dan got down into the river and moved the brick and took out the plastic container. It had been at a safe water level, in spite of the rains, and Fresh was inside, alive and well.

Dan took Fresh out of the carton just to make sure. Then he put him among the stones in the river for the fun of seeing his disappearing act.

As he watched, Dan reflected that this was what Fresh would have done if the fisherman *had* spotted the carton and taken him out of it for a good look, and then by mistake dropped him into the water. The fisherman would have lost sight of him, and Fresh would have buried himself. He would have been gone for good—for good, back into the river.

The only signs would have been the brick moved, the plastic container out of place. And Fresh gone. That was all that Dan could have reported to Laurie.

But it had not happened, after all.

Dan picked up Fresh and put him back in the carton and put the carton back, and then the brick, and then walked home. He told Laurie, sitting in his pyjamas in front of the TV with his supper, that everything had been all right. He did not say more.

On the fifth day, the day before Laurie's return to London, they went together to the riverbank. There was no fisherman. The brick was exactly in place and behind it the plastic carton, with the water flowing through correctly. There was Fresh, safe, sound, and apparently not even pining at captivity.

"Tomorrow," said Laurie. "Tomorrow morning we'll bring the jam jar, ready for me to take him home on the train."

That night was the last of Laurie's visit. He and Dan shared Dan's bedroom, and tonight they went to bed at the same time and fell asleep together.

Dan's father was the last person to go to bed at the end of the evening. He bolted the doors and turned out the last lights. That usually did not wake Dan, but tonight it did. Suddenly he was wide awake in the complete darkness, hearing the sound of his parents going to bed in their room, hearing the sound of Laurie's breathing in the next bed, the slow, whispering breath of deep sleep.

The movements and murmurs from the other bedroom ceased; Laurie's breathing continued evenly. Dan still lay wide awake.

He had never really noticed before how very dark everything could be. It was more than blackness; it seemed to fill space as water fills a pool. It seemed to fill the inside of his head.

He lay for some time with
the darkness everywhere;
then he got up very quietly.
He put trousers and sweater
on over his pyjamas,
bunchily. Laurie's breathing
never changed. He tiptoed
out of the bedroom and
downstairs. In the hall, he
put on his Wellington boots.
He let himself out of the
house and then through the
front gate. There was no one

about, no lights in the houses, except for a night light
where a child slept. There was one lamp in the lane,
and that sent his shadow leaping horribly ahead of
him. Then he turned a corner and the lamplight had
gone. He was taking the short cut towards the river.

No moon tonight. No stars. Darkness . . .

He had been born here; he had always lived here;
he knew these meadows as well as he knew himself;
but the darkness made him afraid. He could not see
the familiar way ahead; he had to remember it. He
felt his way. He scented it. He smelled the river before
he came to it, and he felt the vegetation changing
underfoot, growing ranker when he reached the bank.

He lowered himself into the water, from darkness into darkness. He began to feel along the roots of the bank for the upended brick. He found it quickly—he had not been far out in the point at which he had struck the bank.

His hand was on the brick, and he kept it there while he tried to see. In the darkness and through the darkness, he tried to see what was going to happen— what he was going to make happen. What he was going to do.

Now that he was no longer moving, he could hear the sound of other movements in the darkness. He heard the water flowing. He heard a *drip* of water into water somewhere near him; a long pause; another *drip*. He heard a quick, quiet birdcall that was strange to him; certainly not an owl—he used to hear those as he lay snug in bed in his bedroom at home. And whatever sound he heard now, he heard beneath it the ceaseless, watery, whispering sound of the river, as if the river were alive and breathing in its sleep in the darkness, like Laurie left sleeping in the bedroom at home.

It was within his power to move the brick and take hold of the plastic carton and tip it right over. Fresh would fall into the water with a *plop* so tiny that he might never hear it above the flow of the river. In such darkness, there would be no question of finding Fresh again, ever.

If he meant to do it, he could do it in three seconds. His hand was on the brick.

But did he mean to do it?

He tried to see what was in his mind, but his mind was like a deep pool of darkness. He didn't know what he really meant to do.

Suddenly he took his hand from the brick and stood erect. He put his booted foot on one of the lateral roots that extended behind the brick. He had to feel for it with his toe. Having found it, he pressed it slowly downwards; then quickly took his foot off again.

He could feel the root, released from the pressure, following his foot upwards again in a little jerk.

That jerk of the root might have been enough to upset or at least tilt the carton. It might have been enough to tip Fresh out into the river.

On the other hand, of course, it might not have been enough.

Dan flung himself at the bank well to one side of the brick and clambered up and began a blundering run across the meadows. He did not slow up or go more carefully until he reached the lamplight of the lane and the possibility of someone's hearing his footsteps.

He let himself into the house and secured the door behind him. He left his boots in the hall and his clothes on the chair in the bedroom. He crept back into bed. Laurie was still breathing gently and regularly.

Dan slept late the next morning. He woke to bright sunshine flooding the room and Laurie banging on the bedrail. "Fresh! Fresh! Fresh!" he was chanting. Dan looked at him through eyes half-shut. He was trying to remember a dream he had had last night. It had been a dream of darkness—too dark to remember, or to want to remember. But when he went downstairs to breakfast and saw his boots in the hall with mud still drying on them, he knew that he had not dreamed last night.

Immediately after breakfast, they went down to the river. Laurie was carrying his jam jar.

They climbed down into the shallows as usual. Laurie made a little sound of dismay when he saw the brick. "It's lopsided—the current's moved it!"

Dan stood at a distance in the shallows while Laurie scrabbled the brick down into the water with a splash. There behind it was the white plastic carton, but at a considerable tilt, so that water flowed steadily from its lowest corner. "Oh, Fresh—Fresh!" Laurie implored in a whisper. He was peering into the carton.

"Well?" said Dan, from his distance, not moving.

"Oh, no!" Laurie exclaimed, low but in dismay.

"Well?"

Laurie was poking with a finger at the bottom of the carton. Suddenly he laughed. "He's here after all! It's all right! It was just that burying trick of his! Fresh is here!"

Laurie was beaming.

Dan said, "I'm glad."

Laurie transferred Fresh from the carton to the jam jar, together with some mud and stones and a suitable amount of river water. Dan watched him.

Then they both set off across the meadows again, Laurie holding the jam jar carefully, as he would need to do—as he *would* do—during all the long journey to London. He was humming to himself. He stopped to say to Dan, "I say, I did thank you for Fresh, didn't I?"

"Don't thank me," said Dan.

Theme Introduction

Resourcefulness

In this section of the book, you will read about characters who find clever ways to get what they want or need. Thinking about these stories, and about your own experiences with resourcefulness, will give you new ideas about what it means to be resourceful.

IMPORTANT QUESTIONS TO THINK ABOUT

Before starting this section, think about your own experiences being resourceful:

- Can you think of a time you solved a problem in a new or clever way?

- Think of a problem you had in the past that you now know how to solve. How did you learn to solve the problem?

Once you have thought about your own experiences with resourcefulness, think about this **theme question** and write down your answers or share them aloud:

What does it mean to be resourceful?

After reading each story in this section, ask yourself the theme question again. You may have some new ideas you want to add.

"Your tablespoon gave birth to a teaspoon."

Shrewd Todie and Lyzer the Miser

Ukrainian folktale
as told by Isaac Bashevis Singer

In a village somewhere in Ukraine, there lived a poor man called Todie. Todie had a wife, Shaindel, and seven children, but he could never earn enough to feed them properly. He tried many trades and failed in all of them. It was said of Todie that if he decided to deal in candles the sun would never set. He was nicknamed Shrewd Todie because whenever he managed to make some money, it was always by trickery.

This winter was an especially cold one. The snowfall was heavy, and Todie had no money to buy wood for the stove. His seven children stayed in bed all day to keep warm. When the frost burns outside, hunger is stronger than ever, but Shaindel's larder was empty. She reproached Todie bitterly, wailing, "If you can't feed your wife and children, I will go to the rabbi and get a divorce."

"And what will you do with it, eat it?" Todie retorted.

In the same village there lived a rich man called Lyzer. Because of his stinginess he was known as Lyzer the Miser. He permitted his wife to bake bread only once in four weeks because he had discovered that fresh bread is eaten up more quickly than stale.

Todie had more than once gone to Lyzer for a loan of a few gulden, but Lyzer had always replied, "I sleep better when the money lies in my strongbox rather than in your pocket."

Lyzer had a goat, but he never fed her. The goat had learned to visit the houses of the neighbors, who pitied her and gave her potato peelings. Sometimes, when there were not enough peelings, she would gnaw on the old straw of the thatched roofs. She also had a liking for tree bark. Nevertheless, each year the goat gave birth to a kid. Lyzer milked her but, miser that he was, did not drink the milk himself. Instead he sold it to others.

Todie decided that he would take revenge on Lyzer and at the same time make some much-needed money for himself.

One day, as Lyzer was sitting
on a box eating borscht and dry
bread (he used his chairs only on
holidays so that the upholstery
would not wear out), the door
opened and Todie came in.

"Reb Lyzer," he said, "I
would like to ask you a favor.
My oldest daughter, Basha, is
already fifteen and she's about
to become engaged. A young
man is coming from Janev to look
her over. My cutlery is tin, and my
wife is ashamed to ask the young man to eat soup
with a tin spoon. Would you lend me one of your
silver spoons? I give you my holy word that I will
return it to you tomorrow."

Lyzer knew that Todie would not dare to break a
holy oath, and he lent him the spoon.

No young man came to see Basha that evening.
As usual, the girl walked around barefoot and
in rags, and the silver spoon lay hidden under
Todie's shirt. In the early years of his marriage,
Todie had possessed a set of silver tableware himself.
He had, however, long since sold it all, with the
exception of three silver teaspoons that were used
only on Passover.

The following day, as Lyzer, his feet bare (in order to save his shoes), sat on his box eating borscht and dry bread, Todie returned.

"Here is the spoon I borrowed yesterday," he said, placing it on the table together with one of his own teaspoons.

"What is the teaspoon for?" Lyzer asked.

And Todie said, "Your tablespoon gave birth to a teaspoon. It is her child. Since I am an honest man, I'm returning both mother and child to you."

Lyzer looked at Todie in astonishment. He had never heard of a silver spoon giving birth to another. Nevertheless, his greed overcame his doubt, and he happily accepted both spoons. Such an unexpected piece of good fortune! He was overjoyed that he had loaned Todie the spoon.

A few days later, as Lyzer (without his coat, to save it) was again sitting on his box eating borscht with dry bread, the door opened and Todie appeared.

"The young man from Janev did not please Basha because he had donkey ears, but this evening another young man is coming to look her over. Shaindel is cooking soup for him, but she's ashamed to serve him with a tin spoon. Would you lend me . . ."

60

Even before Todie could finish the sentence, Lyzer interrupted. "You want to borrow a silver spoon? Take it with pleasure."

The following day Todie once more returned the spoon and with it one of his own silver teaspoons. He again explained that during the night the large spoon had given birth to a small one, and in all good conscience he was bringing back the mother and newborn baby. As for the young man who had come to look Basha over, she hadn't liked him either, because his nose was so long that it reached to his chin. Needless to say, Lyzer the Miser was overjoyed.

Exactly the same thing happened a third time. Todie related that this time his daughter had rejected her suitor because he stammered. He also reported that Lyzer's silver spoon had again given birth to a baby spoon.

"Does it ever happen that a spoon has twins?" Lyzer inquired.

Todie thought it over for a moment. "Why not? I've even heard of a case where a spoon had triplets."

Almost a week passed by, and Todie did not go to see Lyzer. But on Friday morning, as Lyzer (in his underdrawers to save his pants) sat on his box eating borscht and dry bread, Todie came in and said, "Good day to you, Reb Lyzer."

"A good morning and many more to you," Lyzer replied in his friendliest manner. "What good fortune brings you here? Did you perhaps come to borrow a silver spoon? If so, help yourself."

"Today I have a very special favor to ask. This evening a young man from the big city of Lublin is coming to look Basha over. He is the son of a rich man, and I'm told he is clever and handsome as well. Not only do I need a silver spoon, but since he will remain with us over the Sabbath, I need a pair of silver candlesticks, because mine are brass and my wife is ashamed to place them

on the Sabbath table. Would you lend me your
candlesticks? Immediately after the Sabbath, I will
return them to you."

Silver candlesticks are of great value and Lyzer the
Miser hesitated, but only for a moment.

Remembering his good fortune with the spoons,
he said, "I have eight silver candlesticks in my house.
Take them all. I know you will return them to me
just as you say. And if it should happen that any of
them give birth, I have no doubt that you will be as
honest as you have been in the past."

"Certainly," Todie said. "Let's hope for the best."

The silver spoon, Todie hid beneath his shirt as usual. But taking the candlesticks, he went directly to a merchant, sold them for a considerable sum, and brought the money to Shaindel. When Shaindel saw so much money, she demanded to know where he had gotten such a treasure.

"When I went out, a cow flew over our roof and dropped a dozen silver eggs," Todie replied. "I sold them and here is the money."

"I have never heard of a cow flying over a roof and laying silver eggs," Shaindel said doubtingly.

"There is always a first time," Todie answered. "If you don't want the money, give it back to me."

"There'll be no talk about giving it back," Shaindel said. She knew that her husband was full of cunning and tricks—but when the children are hungry and the larder is empty, it is better not to ask too many questions. Shaindel went to the marketplace and bought meat, fish, white flour, and even some nuts and raisins for a pudding. And since a lot of money still remained, she bought shoes and clothes for the children.

It was a very gay Sabbath in Todie's house. The boys sang and the girls danced. When the children asked their father where he had gotten the money, he replied, "It is forbidden to mention money during the Sabbath."

Sunday, as Lyzer (barefoot and almost naked
to save his clothes) sat on his box finishing up a
dry crust of bread with borscht, Todie arrived and,
handing him his silver spoon, said, "It's too bad. This
time your spoon did not give birth to a baby."

"What about the candlesticks?" Lyzer inquired
anxiously.

Todie sighed deeply. "The candlesticks died."

Lyzer got up from his box so hastily that he
overturned his plate of borscht.

"You fool! How can candlesticks die?" he
screamed.

"If spoons can give birth, candlesticks can die."

Lyzer raised a great hue and cry and had Todie called before the rabbi. When the rabbi heard both sides of the story, he burst out laughing. "It serves you right," he said to Lyzer. "If you hadn't chosen to believe that spoons give birth, now you would not be forced to believe that your candlesticks died."

"But it's all nonsense," Lyzer objected.

"Did you not expect the candlesticks to give birth to other candlesticks?" the rabbi said admonishingly. "If you accept nonsense when it brings you profit, you must also accept nonsense when it brings you loss." And he dismissed the case.

The following day, when Lyzer the Miser's wife brought him his borscht and dry bread, Lyzer said to her, "I will eat only the bread. Borscht is too expensive a food, even without sour cream."

66

The story of the silver spoons that gave birth and the candlesticks that died spread quickly through the town. All the people enjoyed Todie's victory and Lyzer the Miser's defeat. The shoemaker's and tailor's apprentices, as was their custom whenever there was an important happening, made up a song about it:

Lyzer, put your grief aside.
What if your candlesticks have died?
You're the richest man on earth
With silver spoons that can give birth
And silver eggs as living proof
Of flying cows above your roof.
Don't sit there eating crusts of bread—
To silver grandsons look ahead.

However, time passed and Lyzer's silver spoons never gave birth again.

"I'll fix nets in trade for paint."

ON SAND ISLAND

Jacqueline Briggs Martin

CARL'S POCKETS

When Lake Superior was thick with fish
and strung with nets,
and fishermen found their way on the water
by watching the sun,
a Sand Island boy named Carl
put salt in his pocket every morning.
He knew—because Old Uncle Oliver had told him—
if he could throw salt on a live rabbit's tail
he could make a wish,
and the wish would come true.
That was his good-luck pocket.

69

In his other pocket
he kept the green beach glass
he and his mother had found
four summers ago,
when Carl was only six.
His mother had been gone since last fall,
carried to Bayfield in a coffin
on the roof of a fishing boat.
But Carl had the glass,
rubbed smooth by the lake
and his own hand.
That was his keep-away-bad-luck pocket.

SAND ISLAND LUCK

Bad luck on Sand Island
was a five-day storm,
which meant Carl's father couldn't lift his nets
and pick out the fish caught in their mesh.
Bad luck was a cold, sister-still-sleeping kitchen
when Carl got up in the morning.
Bad luck was getting to Moe's dock too late
to see the *C. W. Turner* drop off the mail.
And bad luck was standing at the edge of the water
when he could be out in a boat.

Good luck on Sand Island was
a big lift of fish in his father's nets.
On those bright days
his father played Norway folk songs
on the harmonica.
His sister put on their mother's best scarf—
the red wool—
and they danced in the kitchen.

Good luck was a piece of Anna Mae Hill's coconut cake—
sweet and crumbly and covered with cream
whipped so thick fishermen said they could stand on it.
Good luck was afternoon rafting along East Bay.
But the best luck for Carl
would be having his own boat.

BOATS

Carl wanted a boat of his own
more than a new bicycle.
A boat could take him out
away from the too-quiet house,
away from his sister's lumpy, no-salt, no-sugar meals.
A boat could take him out
where the quiet was filled
with water and sky.

Carl dreamed about boats.
He drew the boat he would build:
a little flat-bottomed pound boat,
like the fishermen use
who set poles and nets in the lake
to make fences for fish.
"You're too young to build a boat," his sister said.
"It will sink
before you get past Moe's dock.
And we'll lose you, too."

THE BEGINNING

Then came the day
Carl found the boards
floated in off the lake—
long, wide boards
to cut and hammer into a boat.

Hummingbirds ate from jewelweed flowers,
while Carl tugged those boards
up from the beach
to the grass beside his father's fish shed.
That was the end of the hard work,
he told himself.
Sawing would be easy.

WORK FOR WORK

The next morning
Carl's father went out on the water
to drop nets in the place of
"fire in the branches," the place
where he could see the sun through the trees
at Lighthouse Point.
Carl looked at his boards
and imagined himself in his new boat,
rowing so close to ducks
he could count their feathers.

But the saw stuck in the wood
or took quick jumps
and scratched his hands.
Carl couldn't make it cut.
His sister was busy washing clothes.
His father would be out until supper.

Perhaps their neighbor Torvald,
a little man who whistled all day
and built rocking chairs from fish barrels,
would trade work for work.

Torvald said,
"Sure I'll cut your wood,
if you'll pick my strawberries.
The *C. W. Turner* comes tomorrow
and will take them to sell in Bayfield."

Carl picked strawberries all afternoon.
He picked until he thought
he'd always walk a little bit stooped,
like Old Uncle Oliver.
Torvald sawed the wood
and stacked it in a pile.

That night Carl said,
"That's the end of the hard work.
Nailing will be easy."

BURT HILL

The next morning
Carl looked at the pile of boards
and imagined he was boating
in the caves by Swallow Point,
looking for pictures drawn on the rocks
by the First People who lived on Sand Island.

But he was stopped
when he found no nails in the fish shed.
He didn't want to pick strawberries again.
Then Carl thought of Burt Hill.

Burt Hill was a saver. His shop
was filled with scraps of metal, pieces of wood,
and cans of used nails, hinges, bolts, and screws.
The shop's best place was the wall
where Burt wrote down
what he saved for memory:

> *Summer 1910.* Moved to Sand Island. Tore down the old
> fish shed. Used the lumber on the house.

> *November 1911.* Boat broke down twice on the lake.
> Got home—but covered with ice, stem to stern.

> *June 1913.* Capt. Lee towed raft of logs through my
> pound nets and ruined them for the season.

> *May 28, 1914.* Our Marguerite graduated from Bayfield
> High School. We went to watch. M. came home with us.

> *November 1915.* Anna Mae and M. cooked like two steam
> engines for large crew of herring fishermen.

Burt Hill smelled of pipe smoke
and the peppermints
he carried in a small paper bag.
He always let Carl pick candy out of the bag.

"Sure, I've got nails," Burt said.
"Help me move these rocks under my dock
so it won't float away in high water.
Anna Mae won't let you work without lunch.
After we eat we'll go and look at your boat."

They loaded rocks as big as pumpkins
onto the stone drag,
hauled them along the beach,
and dropped them inside the crib,
which would hold them under the dock.

Carl's arms were sore that night.
But he looked at his boat—nailed tight,
and snug with caulking cotton—and said,
"That's the last of the hard work.
Painting will be easy."

KEEPING OUT THE WATER

The next morning
Carl sat in his boat
and saw himself out in Lighthouse Bay,
catching fish for Sunday dinner.
But he needed paint to seal the joints
or his boat would sink
before he got to Lighthouse Bay.
He had no paint.

Perhaps Fred Hansen could help.
The Hansens were neighbors,
and island neighbors are closer than cousins.
Carl found the fisherman busy with nets.
"I'll fix nets," the boy said, "in trade for paint."
So they sewed cedar floats—corks—
to a line at the top of the nets
and pounded lead weights to a line at the bottom.
The nets, made of string
fine enough for a baby's hat,
would stand straight in the water—
invisible snags for whitefish and trout.

By the time they finished, Carl thought
he would see fishnets
whenever he closed his eyes.

But just before supper,
he looked at his boat,
sealed and shiny with paint,
and said,
"That's the end of the hard work."

THE OLD OARS

The next morning
spiders made webs on thimbleberry leaves.
Carl's sister churned cream into butter.
Carl's father said,
"That's a right boat you've built.
But you'll need some oars."
He went to a back corner of the fish shed
and found two oars.
"These are old—from Norway.
You can clean them up
while your paint dries and cures."

Carl sanded off the dirt and bad wood.
He thought he could have sandpapered the entire fish shed
in the time it took him to fix up those splintery oars.
As the sun was setting
off Lighthouse Point,
Carl said, "That's the last of the hard work."

And he was right.

BOAT CELEBRATION

In the morning
Carl walked to the water and looked at his boat.
His sister had come before him
and set up their mother's red scarf for a flag.

While island rabbits ate grass under bushes
Carl took the boat out on the water.
He rowed close enough to ducks in the Easy Bay
to count their feathers.
He rowed next to the caves
and looked for secret pictures
from the First People.
He caught three fish
as long as his arm.

His father said they should celebrate
the newest boat on the island.
His sister made Carl's favorite stew
of fish and butter and milk.
She asked Carl to add salt from his good-luck pocket.

Burt and Anna Mae Hill
came with coconut cream cake.
Fred Hansen and his family
came with bustle and warm bread.
Old Uncle Oliver came with a fiddle.
Neighbor Torvald came with strawberry jam.

They ate together,
danced, and sang,
and everyone said Carl would make a fine boatman.

Then they went home to sleep
and wait for the sun to rise
on another day on Sand Island.

The forest creatures were not afraid of him.

THE GREEN MAN

Gail E. Haley

The story you are about to read may have happened just this way—or perhaps it came about in a different manner in some other place entirely. . . .

Claude was the only son of Squire Archibald. He was arrogant, vain, and selfish. He spent most of his time hunting, hawking, and riding about the countryside in his fine clothes.

One evening Claude rode into the village, and after ordering a lavish meal at the Mermaid and Bush, he sat watching the bustle of village life.

"Look at those ignorant peasants putting food out for the Green Man when they can barely feed their own children."

"They are grateful, Master Claude," replied the landlord. "For the Green Man keeps their animals healthy. He protects their children if they stray into the forest. Without him, the crops would not grow, nor the seasons turn in their course."

"Rubbish! Those are just silly tales. There is no Green Man!"

"Mind your tongue, sir," chided the landlord. "Terrible things can happen to those who make fun of old beliefs."

Some days afterward, Claude set out for a day's hunting. He never hunted on foot; he preferred to shoot from horseback. His men and dogs had gone ahead as beaters to drive the game toward him, but nothing was happening, and Claude grew tired of waiting. He rode deeper into the forest.

"Those beaters are incompetent. I haven't seen an animal all day!" he grumbled.

Soon Claude was hopelessly lost. It was hot, and his clothes felt heavy, when through the trees he saw a shady pond. Tethering his horse to a tree, he stripped off his clothes and dived into the cool water. He did not see a thin bony hand reaching out of the bushes.

Claude came out of the water refreshed and hungry, but on the bank he found nothing but a coil of rope.

Claude tied some leafy branches around his waist with the rope. Then he ate some of the strawberries that were growing on the bank. Feeling better, he chose a stout branch as a walking stick and set off to find his way home. But as the day drew to a close, Claude realized that he would have to spend the night in the forest.

Peering about in the gloom, he saw before him the entrance to a large cave and felt his way inside. As he grew accustomed to the dark, Claude realized that he was not alone. There seemed to be something with glittering eyes and sharp horns near the mouth of the cave.

"Stay back! I'm armed!" Claude shouted. But the creature came no closer. Then something moved near the back of the cave. Claude clutched his stick for protection and drew his legs up onto a ledge. He lay there until, exhausted, he fell asleep.

When Claude woke it was morning and a little
nanny goat was standing before him, tossing her
head. He laughed with relief. It must have been she
who had been at the back of the cave in the night.

Claude looked around. A young rooster was
pecking busily near a nest full of eggs. A clay jug and
a stone ax hung on the wall above Claude's head.
Several rough baskets stood on the floor, and there
was ash from a recent fire.

"'This is someone's home," thought Claude.
"Perhaps I should feed the animals." He gave the hens
some grain which he found in a bowl and picked
some fresh grass for the goat as a special treat. Then
he helped himself to goat's milk and eggs.

The goat nuzzled his hand, and he scratched her behind the ears. She frisked about and followed him when he set off to explore.

Not far away, Claude found a bees' nest in a tree, its honeycomb shining from inside the hollow trunk. Covering his body with mud to protect himself from stings, he climbed up to collect some honey.

Just then, a party of his father's men broke through the trees, blowing their horns and hallooing for him.

"They'll think I've gone mad, if they see me sitting in a tree covered with mud," thought Claude. "I can't let them see me without my clothes and my boots. I would be disgraced!"

So he let the party pass without revealing himself. Then he climbed down from the tree and crept back to the cave, followed all the time by the goat.

"I'll borrow something to cover myself from the owner of the cave when he returns, and then I'll set off for home again," Claude said to his new friend, the goat. But time passed, and no one came. Claude lived on in the cave, growing leaner and stronger every day.

As the warm days went by, Claude forgot altogether about clothes. He nearly forgot that he was Claude, the Squire's son. He became Milker-of-the-Goat, Feeder-of-the-Hens, Friend-of-All-Wild-Animals. The forest creatures were not afraid of him. He fed them, talked to them, and spent hours watching them hunt and play.

As the berries, fruits, and nuts ripened, Claude became Gatherer-and-Preserver. When the grain was harvested in distant fields, he became Gleaner, venturing out at night to gather the leftovers for himself and his animals.

Claude was enjoying his new life. Even the sun and the moon seemed to smile upon him.

One morning, after a heavy rainstorm, Claude heard a frantic bellow coming from the direction of the river. He hurried there to see what was wrong, and found a cow who had been separated from her calf. They had taken shelter from the rain in a hilltop thicket, and as the water rose the river had surrounded them, turning the hillock into an island. The terrified calf would not follow its mother through the swirling current, and the cow was mooing loudly for help.

Claude waded across the water, picked up the calf, and carried it to its mother. Gratefully, the cow licked his hand and then led her calf away through the forest toward the safety of the farmyard.

As the days grew colder, Claude added more ivy leaves to his costume. He tucked strips of moss and lichen between them to keep out the cold. He pounded birch bark to make it soft, and sewed pieces together to make a curtain for the mouth of the cave. After several attempts he even succeeded in making himself some birch-bark boots.

He built a fireplace near the entrance. He had found stones the right size and shape to make a mortar and a pestle, and each day he ground grain or nuts or acorns into flour. The smell of baking bread filled the air. A family of hedgehogs moved in.

The cave was now well stocked with food. Strings of mushrooms, parsnips, wild onions, and herbs hung

on drying poles. Claude made slings for the fruit and
vegetables he had gathered. He formed barrels out of
bark to hold apples and roots. Baskets of nuts, grain,
and seeds were stored on a shelf above his mossy bed.

One day when Claude was out gathering acorns,
he encountered a fierce wild boar threatening two
small children from the village.

"Don't be such a selfish swine!" Claude spoke firmly
to the boar. "There are enough acorns for everyone.
Go away and let the children have their share."

The boar snorted defiantly but turned and trotted
back into the forest.

"There, there, don't cry.
The old boar is gone now,"
Claude comforted the
children.

The girl looked up through her tears at the tall, sunburned man. He seemed as ancient, green, and moss-covered as the oak tree that towered above them.

"Are you the Green Man?" she asked in a whisper.

Claude looked down in surprise. Warm sunshine caressed his hair. A gentle breeze rippled his leafy costume. His feet felt as if they were rooted in the earth.

"Yes," Claude answered her at last, "I am the Green Man."

He helped the children to gather up their acorns and filled their basket to the brim. Then he led them safely to the edge of the forest.

When winter came, at night Claude visited the nearby sleeping villages. He helped himself to some of the food put out for him but always left some for hungry, prowling animals. At times he felt lonely as he walked through the deserted streets, looking into the windows of the cozy houses. He was homesick for his own village and his family. But he returned each night to his cave and his animals. He was needed now in the forest.

Winter passed and spring was on its way. The smell of budding leaves, warm earth, and growing things filled the air. The days went by, and when he knew that the strawberries would be ripening by the pond, Claude went to pick them.

A man was splashing in the water. A fine suit of clothing lay on the bank and a handsome horse was tethered nearby.

Claude quietly took off his leaves and put on the clothes. He found shears and a glass in the horse's saddlebag, so he cut his long hair and trimmed his beard. Then he rode through the forest until he found his own home.

His mother and father were amazed and delighted to see him. Everyone thought that he had been killed long ago by robbers or eaten by wild animals.

"It was the Green Man who saved my life," was all that Claude would say.

His year away had changed the arrogant young man. Now he was hospitable to travelers. He cared for his animals. And each night Claude set out food and drink for the Green Man.

Theme Introduction

Communication

In this section of the book, you'll read about characters who find different ways to express their thoughts and feelings. Thinking about these stories, and about your own experiences, will give you new ideas about the different ways people communicate.

Important Questions to Think About

Before starting this section, think about your own experiences communicating with others:

- Can you think of a time when you communicated well with someone? What made it go well?

- Think of a time when someone didn't understand something important that you were trying to tell him or her. What did you do to help the person understand?

Once you have thought about your own experiences with communication, think about this **theme question** and write down your answers or share them aloud:

What makes communication successful and what makes it unsuccessful?

After reading each story in this section, ask yourself the theme question again. You may have some new ideas you want to add.

My mother, she doesn't understand at all.

SONG OF HOPE

Peggy Duffy

My mother, she doesn't understand at all.

I tell her, Coach says if we don't come to soccer practice, we don't get to play in the game on Sunday.

She says, "I need you come shopping with me." I nod my head and obey. It is Korean way. Come Sunday I sit on the bench, hanging my head, wanting more than anything to get my foot on the ball. The final score is one to one. Tie game. I know if the coach had put me out on the field, I would have helped score a goal.

After the game, Coach says, "Coming to practice tomorrow?"

"Yes," I say.

When I get home, I take off my cleats and leave them outside the door beside the new navy blue shoes I helped my mother buy last week. I told the man which ones she wanted to try on, what size she wore, which pair she finally decided to buy. I counted out the money and made sure she got the correct change.

"How was the game?" my mother asks. She is at the kitchen sink draining salted water from chopped cabbage for kimchi.

"Okay. How was church?" I say.

She never comes to the games. Sunday is church day. I go to church in the morning, but my mother stays all day. Everyone in church speaks Korean. Sunday is why after three years in the United States my mother has never learned to speak English. No more than a few words. *Hello. Yes, please. Thank you very much.* She makes do by smiling and nodding her head like a bouncy ball, pretending she understands.

My mother, she doesn't understand at all.

I was in the sixth grade when we moved here for Father's job. "You get to learn English," my grandmother said when she kissed me goodbye at the airport. "How lucky is that?"

Not lucky at all. I wasn't placed in a regular classroom. I was placed in a special class. No one else in the class spoke Korean. No one but the teacher spoke English. All day long we colored pictures. Pictures of houses. Pictures of family. Pictures of food. There were lines and loops printed beneath each picture. "These are letters," the special teacher said. "These letters make words."

I didn't learn English in the special class. I didn't learn English from Father who works long days and comes home too tired to speak even in Korean with me and Mother.

I learned English from watching TV. I learned that my last name, Song, is American word for music. I like American music. More than anything, I wanted to know what their songs said. So every day after school I sat in front of the TV. One day it clicked what all those words meant. Americans sing of love. They sing of heartbreak. They sing of hope. They don't sing of obedience.

My teacher was so proud. She moved me into the regular class. My mother was so happy. She no longer needed to point to what she wanted at the store. She had me to talk.

At the sink my mother holds the cabbage under running water to rinse off the salt. She washes each piece three times. "Tomorrow I have errands to run," she says in Korean.

"Tomorrow I have soccer practice," I say in same language.

"Why always soccer practice?"

"Coach say," I tell her. I think she should understand such loyalty. But I forget. She gives me a look to help me remember. I am only child. I am also oldest daughter. Oldest daughter's responsibility is first to mother.

"Please, Coach won't let me play if I don't go," I say.

"Is not so important, this game," she says. She tightens her lips and goes to work mixing green onions with garlic, chiles, ginger, and water. Then she pours the mixture over the cabbage and stirs everything up in a big crock. A scowl is etched into her face, and her eyes disappear beneath tiny folds of skin. She thinks I should play the violin or the cello and be in the school orchestra. Or twirl around in a leotard in front of a wall of mirrors at dancing school and be in a recital on stage.

But I am a big girl, not little like she. I am stocky girl, thickset like Grandfather way back in Father's family. My fingers are too wide to press on one violin string without causing the one next to it to squawk like the geese we feed in the park, my feet too clumsy to stand long on toes for ballet. I topple over to one side. But I am a good soccer player. I run fast and have what Coach calls "a big foot" that can kick the ball far up the field. He says I have a good chance of making the high school varsity team in a few years, but I need lots of play time with my club team. I want to tell this to my mother, but I don't know how to make her understand. I don't even know Korean word for varsity.

"There," my mother says, spooning the cabbage mixture into a large jar. "In a few days' time we have kimchi."

"In one day's time I have soccer practice."

"When?"

"Four o'clock."

She lowers a lid onto the jar. "Not done with errands by four o'clock."

I lower my eyes to the floor.

In English I say, "Thank you, thank you very much." I say it in a way that Americans call sarcastic, but I say it very soft, under my breath, so far under that I know the words will not rise to my mother's ears.

I do not want to disobey my mother, but if I don't go to practice tomorrow, there is no hope of me playing in the game and that would break my heart. So I do a very disobedient thing. When I leave for school the next day, I slip my cleats and shin guards into my backpack along with my books.

After school I go to the field and wait for everyone else to show up. Coach says, "Well Miss Song, I see you've finally decided to make a commitment to the team."

"Yes," I say. There's a note of that American sarcasm in his voice, but I pretend I don't hear it.

I practice hard. It is a hot day, the air sticky like fresh steamed rice. Sweat clings to my face. We practice drills for over an hour—foot skill drills, sprinting drills, give-and-go passing drills. Coach

announces one last drill. I pass the ball, wipe the hot
salty sweat from my eyes and see my mother at the
edge of the field, umbrella held high to keep the sun
off her face. Even from this distance, I can't miss the
scowl etched deep into the corners of her mouth. I
run up the field to receive a pass, kick with the inside
of my foot, but my timing is
off. The ball boomerangs
off my cleat and lands
out of bounds.

Coach calls us off the field and divides us into two
groups for a scrimmage. He nods his head toward
where my mother stands. I don't look like my mother,
but I am the only Korean girl on the team. It is easy
for Coach to figure out whose mother she is.

Coach says, "She here to pick you up?"

"Yes," I say.

"Okay, fifteen more minutes and you can go."

But after the scrimmage, Coach decides we need to run. He tells us to do four laps around the field. I run as hard as I can, pumping my legs so fast and hard they hurt, breathing even faster and harder until my lungs seem to gasp for air all on their own and my chest doesn't seem big enough to hold them. I run through all that pain. In a game it will be hot and tiring too, and I don't want to let my team down. I don't want to let my mother down either, but it is too late. I already have. I see the disappointment in her face each time I run past where she is standing behind the goal line.

When I finish the last lap, I see Coach walking toward my mother. I run over and beat him to her, still breathing hard, the sweat wet on my skin. My mother gives me a hard look, her lips held in a tight line, but then her face grows softer, eyes appearing again, as the Coach catches up to us.

Coach says, "So you're Tina's mom. It's good to meet you." He offers his hand.

My mother knows this American custom. She places her hand in his and shakes.

"Hello," she says, the big, toothy smile fixed on her mouth like it was painted on. I welcome a slight breeze, feel it dry the sweat on me, cooling my skin.

Coach says, "I'm glad to
have Tina on my team.
She's strong and fast and
not afraid of the ball.
And can she ever kick!"

My mother nods her
head, teeth still showing.
She is all white, like a
soccer ball, with her pale
skin the sun never shines
on and her light teeth.
"Thank you, thank you
very much."

"Now we have to
see about getting her
to practice more,"
Coach says.

My mother nods again. The smile on her face
stretches until the corners of her lips rise to the
bottom of her ears, and her eyes look like two skinny
caterpillars drawn in black crayon across the middle
of her face. "Yes, please," she finally says.

Coach stands there for a long awkward silence.
I know this silence.

"My mother doesn't understand," I say. He looks
at me with his own frown of not understanding.

"She doesn't speak English," I add.

"Tell her I'm very glad to meet her and I think you are a good soccer player," he says, speaking very slowly and much too loud. I know this custom too. People always talk in this manner when they need me to translate. Like I can't hear if they don't raise their voices. Like I can't remember the words if they don't string them together with big empty spaces in between. I feel my face turn hot, even hotter than it felt running around the field.

My mother looks at me, waiting to hear what Coach has said. Very soft and fast, I tell her. My mother nods at Coach and says, "Thank you. Thank you very much." Her face is red and getting redder, but not from the sun. Not from the heat of running. Red like I have never seen on my mother's face.

Like she doesn't know anything just because she doesn't know English.

I turn and say something to her in Korean, not so softly this time. She says something back. Coach looks like he is waiting for me to translate again, but these words are only for my mother and me. I say something else to her and she smiles, but it is not painted-on smile.

What did I say? I said, "I'd like to see him try and speak Korean."

And she said, "It is not so easy to learn a language when you are old."

And I said, "You are not old. It just takes work and time, like to make kimchi. And you have me to teach you English. How lucky is that?"

Pretty lucky, from the smile on her face.

On the way to the car, she says, "Coach is not so nice. You really want to play soccer with him?"

"I love to play soccer," I say. "And this is the only chance I have to make the high school team one day."

She nods her head like maybe she understands. Then I think, this is America. Here you can fall in love and get your heart broken, but there is always hope. So I say, "Next week I have a game on Saturday."

"Maybe," she says, "Maybe I come to game on Saturday."

"Thank you, thank you very much," I say, in the way Americans call sincere.

109

Jean Labadie was the most popular storyteller.

Jean Labadie's Big Black Dog

French-Canadian folktale
as told by Natalie Savage Carlson

Once in another time, Jean Labadie was the most popular storyteller in the parish. He acted out every story so that it would seem more real.

When he told about the great falls in Niagara, he made a booming noise deep in his throat and whirled his fists around each other. Then each listener could plainly hear the falls and see the white water churning and splashing as if it were about to pour down on his own head. But Jean Labadie had to stop telling his stories about the *loup-garou,* the demon who takes the shape of a terrible animal and pounces upon those foolish people who go out alone at night. Every time the storyteller dropped down on all fours, rolled his eyes, snorted, and clawed at the floor, his listeners ran away from him in terror.

It was only on the long winter evenings that Jean had time to tell these tales. All the rest of the year, he worked hard with his cows and his pigs and his chickens.

One day Jean Labadie noticed that his flock of chickens was getting smaller and smaller. He began to suspect that his neighbor, André Drouillard, was stealing them. Yet he never could catch André in the act.

For three nights running, Jean took his gun down from the wall and slept in the henhouse with his chickens. But the only thing that happened was that his hens were disturbed by having their feeder roost with them, and they stopped laying well. So Jean sighed and put his gun back and climbed into his own bed again.

One afternoon when Jean went to help his neighbor mow the weeds around his barn, he found a bunch of gray chicken feathers near the fence. Now he was sure that André was taking his chickens, for all of his neighbor's chickens were scrawny white things.

He did not know how to broach the matter to André without making an enemy of him. And when one lives in the country and needs help with many tasks, it is a great mistake to make an enemy of a close neighbor. Jean studied the matter as his scythe went swish, swish through the tall weeds. At last he thought of a way out.

112

"Have you seen my big black dog, André?" he
asked his neighbor.

"What big black dog?" asked André. "I didn't
know you had a dog."

"I just got him from the Indians," said Jean.
"Someone has been stealing my chickens so I got
myself a dog to protect them. He is a very fierce dog,
bigger than a wolf and twice as wild."

Jean took one hand off the scythe and pointed to
the ridge behind the barn.

"There he goes now," he cried, "with his big red
tongue hanging out of his mouth. See him!"

André looked but could see nothing.

"Surely you must see him. He runs along so fast.
He lifts one paw this way and another paw that way."

As Jean said this, he dropped the scythe and lifted
first one hand in its black glove and then the other.

André looked at the black gloves
going up and down like the
paws of a big black dog.
Then he looked toward the
ridge. He grew excited.

"Yes, yes," he cried, "I do
see him now. He is running
along the fence. He
lifts one paw this
way and another
paw that way, just
like you say."

Jean was pleased that he was such a good actor he
could make André see a dog that didn't exist at all.

"Now that you have seen him," he said, "you will
know him if you should meet. Give him a wide path
and don't do anything that will make him suspicious.
He is a very fierce watchdog."

André promised to stay a safe distance from the
big black dog.

Jean Labadie was proud of himself over the success
of his trick. No more chickens disappeared. It seemed
that his problem was solved.

Then one day André greeted him with, "I saw
your big black dog in the road today. He was running
along lifting one paw this way and another paw that
way. I got out of his way, you can bet my life!"

Jean Labadie was pleased and annoyed at the same time. Pleased that André believed so completely in the big black dog that he could actually see him. He was also annoyed because the big black dog had been running down the road when he should have been on the farm.

Another day André leaned over the fence.

"Good day, Jean Labadie," he said. "I saw your big black dog on the other side of the village. He was jumping over fences and bushes. Isn't it a bad thing for him to wander so far away? Someone might take him for the *loup-garou*."

Jean Labadie was disgusted with his neighbor's good imagination.

"André," he asked, "how can my dog be on the other side of the village when he is right here at home? See him walking through the yard, lifting one paw this way and another paw that way?"

André looked in Jean's yard with surprise.

"And so he is," he agreed. "My faith, what a one he is! He must run like lightning to get home so fast. Perhaps you should chain him up. Someone will surely mistake such a fast dog for the *loup-garou*."

Jean shrugged hopelessly.

"All right," he said, "perhaps you are right. I will chain him near the henhouse."

"They will be very happy to hear that in the village," said André. "Everyone is afraid of him. I have told them all about him, how big and fierce he is, how his long red tongue hangs out of his mouth, and how he lifts one paw this way and another paw that way."

Jean was angry.

"I would thank you to leave my dog alone, André Drouillard," he said stiffly.

"Oh, ho, and that I do," retorted André. "But today on the road he growled and snapped at me. I would not be here to tell the story if I hadn't taken to a tall maple tree."

Jean Labadie pressed his lips together.

"Then I will chain him up this very moment." He gave a long low whistle. "Come, fellow! Here, fellow!"

André took to his heels.

Of course, this should have ended the matter, and Jean Labadie thought that it had. But one day when he went to the village to buy some nails for his roof, he ran into Madame Villeneuve in a great how-does-it-make of excitement.

"Jean Labadie," she cried to him, "you should be ashamed of yourself, letting that fierce dog run loose in the village."

"But my dog is chained up in the yard at home," said Jean.

"So André Drouillard told me," said Madame, "but he has broken loose. He is running along lifting

116

one paw this way and another paw that way, with
the broken chain dragging in the dust. He growled
at me and bared his fangs. It's a lucky thing his
chain caught on a bush or I would not be talking to
you now."

Jean sighed.

"Perhaps I should get rid of my big black dog,"
he said. "Tomorrow I will take him back to the
Indians."

So next day Jean hitched his horse to the cart
and waited until he saw André Drouillard at work
in his garden. Then he whistled loudly toward the
yard, made a great show of helping his dog climb up
between the wheels and drove past André's house
with one arm curved out in a bow, as if it were
around the dog's neck.

117

"*Au revoir,* André!" he called. Then he looked at the empty half of the seat. "Bark goodbye to André Drouillard, fellow, for you are leaving here forever."

Jean drove out to the Indian village and spent the day with his friends, eating and talking. It seemed a bad waste of time when there was so much to be done on the farm, but on the other hand, it was worth idling all day in order to end the big black dog matter.

Dusk was falling as he rounded the curve near his home. He saw the shadowy figure of André Drouillard waiting for him near his gate. A feeling of foreboding came over Jean.

"What is it?" he asked his neighbor. "Do you have some bad news for me?"

"It's about your big black dog," said André. "He has come back home. Indeed he beat you by an hour. It was that long ago I saw him running down the road to your house with his big red tongue hanging out of his mouth and lifting one paw this way and another paw that way."

Jean was filled with rage. For a twist of tobacco, he would have struck André with his horsewhip.

"André Drouillard," he shouted, "you are a liar! I just left the big black dog with the Indians. They have tied him up."

André sneered.

"A liar am I? We shall see who is the liar. Wait until the others see your big black dog running around again."

So Jean might as well have accused André of being a chicken thief in the first place, for now they were enemies anyway. And he certainly might as well have stayed home and fixed his roof.

Things turned out as his neighbor had hinted. Madame Villeneuve saw the big black dog running behind her house. Henri Dupuis saw him running around the corner of the store. Delphine Langlois even saw him running through the graveyard among the tombstones. And always as he ran along, he lifted one paw this way and another paw that way.

There came that day when Jean Labadie left his neighbor chopping wood all by himself, because they were no longer friends, and drove into the village to have his black mare shod. While he was sitting in front of the blacksmith shop, André Drouillard came galloping up at a great speed.

He could scarcely hold the reins, for one hand was cut and bleeding.

A crowd quickly gathered.

"What is wrong, André Drouillard?" they asked.

"Have you cut yourself?"

"Where is Dr. Brisson? Someone fetch Dr. Brisson."

André Drouillard pointed his bleeding hand at Jean Labadie.

"His big black dog bit me," he accused. "Without warning, he jumped the fence as soon as Jean drove away and sank his teeth into my hand."

There was a gasp of horror from every throat. Jean Labadie reddened. He walked over to André and stared at the wound.

"It looks like an ax cut to me," he said.

Then everyone grew angry at Jean Labadie and his big black dog. They threatened to drive them both out of the parish.

"My friends," said Jean wearily, "I think it is time for this matter to be ended. The truth of it is that I have no big black dog. I never had a big black dog. It was all a joke."

"Aha!" cried André. "Now he is trying to crawl out of the blame. He says he has no big black dog. Yet I have seen it with my own eyes, running around and lifting one paw this way and another paw that way."

"I have seen it, too," cried Madame Villeneuve. "It ran up and growled at me."

"And I."

"And I."

Jean Labadie bowed his head.

"All right, my friends," he said. "There is nothing more I can do about it. I guess that big black dog will eat me out of house and home for the rest of my life."

"You mean you won't make things right about this hand?" demanded André Drouillard.

"What do you want me to do?" asked Jean.

"I will be laid up for a week at least," said André Drouillard, "and right at harvest time. Then, too, there may be a scar. But for two of your plumpest pullets, I am willing to overlook the matter and be friends again."

121

"That is fair," cried Henri Dupuis.

"It is just," cried the blacksmith.

"A generous proposal," agreed everyone.

"And now we will return to my farm," said Jean Labadie, "and I will give André two of my pullets. But all of you must come. I want witnesses."

A crowd trooped down the road to watch the transaction.

After Jean had given his neighbor two of his best pullets, he commanded the crowd, "Wait!"

He went into the house. When he returned, he was carrying his gun.

"I want witnesses," explained Jean, "because I am going to shoot my big black dog. I want everyone to see this happen."

The crowd murmured and surged. Jean gave a long low whistle toward the henhouse.

"Here comes my big black dog," he pointed.

"You can see how he runs to me with his big red tongue hanging out and lifting one paw this way and another paw that way."

Everyone saw the big black dog.

Jean Labadie lifted his gun to his shoulder, pointed it at nothing and pulled the trigger. There was a deafening roar and the gun kicked Jean to the ground. He arose and brushed off his blouse. Madame Villeneuve screamed and Delphine Langlois fainted.

"There," said Jean, brushing away a tear, "it is done. That is the end of my big black dog. Isn't that true?"

And everyone agreed that the dog was gone for good.

Dorobo stirred and shivered in his sleep.

THUNDER, ELEPHANT, AND DOROBO

African folktale
as told by Humphrey Harman

The people of Africa say that if you go to the end of a tree (they mean the top) you find more branches than a man can count, but if you go to the beginning (they mean the bottom) you just find two or three, and that is much easier. Nowadays, they say, we are at the end, and there are so many people and so many things that a man doesn't know where to turn for the clutter the world is in, but that in the beginning things were simpler, and fewer, and a man could see between them. For in the beginning there was only the Earth, and on the Earth were just three important things.

The Earth was much as it is now except that
there was nothing on it which had been *made*. Only
the things that *grow*. If you go into a corner of a
forest very early on a warm misty morning then you
might get some idea of what the world was like then.
Everything very still and vague round the edges, just
growing, quietly.

And in this kind of world were three important
things.

First there was Elephant. He was very shiny and
black because it was a rather wet world, and he
lived in the forest where it is always wet. The mist
collected on his cold white tusks and dripped slowly
off the tips. Sometimes he trampled slowly through
the forest, finding leaves and bark and elephant grass
and wild figs and wild olives to eat, and sometimes
he stood, very tall, very secret, just thinking and
listening to the deep, dignified noises in his stomach.
When he flapped his great ears it was a gesture, no
more. There were no flies.

Then there was Thunder. He was much bigger
than Elephant. He was black also, but not a shiny
black like Elephant. Sometimes there were streaks
of white about him, the kind of white that you get
on the belly of a fish. And he had no *shape*. Or,
rather, one moment he had one shape, and the next
another shape. He was always collecting himself

in and spreading himself out like a huge jellyfish.
And he didn't walk, he rolled along. He was noisy.
Sometimes his voice was very far away, and then
it was not so much a sound as a shaking, which
Elephant could feel coming up from the ground. It
made the drops of mist fall off the leaves and patter
on his broad back. But sometimes, when Thunder
was in his tight shape, his voice cracked high and
angrily, and then Elephant would start and snort and
wheel away deeper into the forest. Not because he
was frightened, but because it hurt his ears.

And last there was Dorobo.

Dorobo is a man, and if you want to see Dorobo you have to go to Africa, because he lives there still. Even then you won't see him very often because he keeps on the edges of places, and most people like to stay in the middle. He lives where the gardens fade out and the forests begin; he lives where the plains stop and the mountains begin, where the grass dries up and the deserts take over. If you want to see him you had better come quickly, because as more and more things are made there is less and less room for Dorobo. He likes to keep himself to himself, and he's almost over the edge.

He is a small man but very stocky. He is the kind of brown that is almost yellow, and he borrows other people's languages to save himself the

bother of making up one of his own. He is always looking steadily for small things that are good at hiding, and because of this the skin round his eyes is crinkled. He makes fire by twirling a pointed stick between the palms of his hands, and then he bends his face sideways and just breathes on a pinch of dried leaf powder and it burns. Fire is about the only thing he does make.

He is very simple and wise, and he was wise then too, when the world was beginning, and he shared it with Elephant and Thunder.

Now these three things were young and new in those days, not quite certain of themselves and rather suspicious of the others because they very seldom met. There was so much room.

One day Thunder came to see Elephant, and after he had rumbled and swelled he settled into the shape that soothed him most, and said, "It's about Dorobo."

Elephant shifted his weight delicately from one foot to the other and said nothing. His ears flapped encouragingly.

"This Dorobo," Thunder went on, "is a strange creature. In fact, so strange that . . . I am leaving the Earth, because I am afraid of him."

Elephant stopped rocking and gurgled with surprise.

"Why?" he asked. "He seems harmless enough to me."

"Listen, Elephant," said Thunder. "When you are sleeping and you get uncomfortable and need to turn upon your other side, what do you do?"

Elephant pondered this. "I stand up," he said at last. "I stand up, and then I lie down again on my other side."

"Well, Dorobo doesn't," said Thunder. "I know. I've watched him. He rolls over without waking up. It's ugly and very strange, and it makes me uncomfortable. The sky, I think, will be a safer home for me."

And Thunder went there. He went straight up, and he's been there ever since. Elephant heard his grumbling die away, and he sucked in his cheeks with astonishment. Then he went to find Dorobo.

It took him three days, but he found him at last, asleep beneath a thorn tree with the grass curled beneath him, like the form of a hare. Elephant rolled slowly forward until he stood right over the sleeping man, and Dorobo lay in his gigantic shadow.

Elephant watched him and pondered over all that Thunder had said.

Presently Dorobo stirred and shivered in his sleep. Then he sighed and then he rolled over and

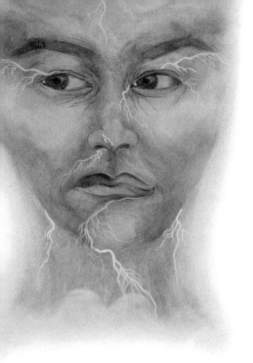

curled himself tighter. It was precisely as Thunder had described.

Elephant had never noticed it before. It was strange indeed, but not, he thought, dangerous.

Dorobo opened his eyes and stared up at Elephant and smiled.

"You are clever, Elephant," he said. "I didn't hear you come. You move so silently."

Elephant said nothing.

Dorobo sat up and put his arms round his knees.

"I'm glad you came," he went on. "I've been wanting to speak to you. Do you know Thunder has left us?"

"I had heard that he had gone," replied Elephant.

"Yes," said Dorobo, "I heard him yesterday in the sky. I'm glad and grateful that he's gone, for, to tell you the truth, I was afraid of Thunder. So big, so loud; and you never knew where he might bob up next. Or in what shape. I like things definite."

"He *was* noisy," said Elephant.

"Now you, Elephant, you're quite different. So quiet and kind. Just think, Elephant, now in the whole world there is just you and me, and we shall get on well together because we understand each other."

Then Elephant laughed. He didn't mean to. It rumbled up inside him and took him by surprise. He threw up his trunk and trumpeted. "This ridiculous little creature!"

Then he was ashamed of his bad manners, and he wheeled ponderously and smashed off into the forest, shaking his great head, shaken by enormous bellows of laughter.

"Yes," he shouted back over his shoulder, "we understand . . . ha, ha! . . . understand one another . . . very . . . well!"

He was a good-natured animal, and he didn't want Dorobo to see that he was laughing at him.

But Dorobo had seen, and although the smile stayed on his face, his eyes were very cold and hard and black, like wet pebbles.

Presently he too slipped into the forest, but he walked slowly and looked carefully about him, and after a while he saw the tree he wanted. It was an old white olive tree, a twisted, slow-growing thing, with a very hard, tough wood. Dorobo searched that tree, and after a long time he found a branch that was straight enough and he bent and twisted it until it broke off.

Then he skinned it with his teeth and trimmed it and laid it in the shade to dry. Then he found thin, strong vines hanging from tall trees like rope from a mast, and he tore them down and trailed them behind him to the river. There he soaked them and beat them into cords against the river rocks, and plaited them very tightly together. When his cord was long enough he took his wild olive branch, which was dry now, and strung the first bow. And he bent the bow almost double and let it go, and it sang for him. Next he found straight, stiff sticks, and he made a fire and burned the end of his sticks a little, and rubbed the charred wood off in the sand. This gave them very hard, sharp points.

Taking his bow and his arrows, he ran to the edge of the desert and found the candelabra tree. The candelabra is a strange tree. It has thick, dull green branches that bear no leaves. And the branches stick up in bunches, a little bent, like the fingers of an old man's hand. And when a branch breaks, and it does very easily, it bleeds a white, sticky sap that drips slowly on the sand. You must never shelter beneath a candelabra tree because if the sap drips in your eyes you go blind.

Dorobo broke a branch and dipped his arrows into the thick, milky sap, and twisted them like a spoon in syrup. Then he laid each carefully against a stone to dry.

When everything was ready he went in search of Elephant.

Elephant was asleep under a fig tree, but he woke up when he heard Dorobo's footsteps in the undergrowth. There was something in the way Dorobo walked—something secret and unfriendly that Elephant did not like. For the first time in his life he felt afraid. As quickly as he could he got to his feet and made off through the forest. Dorobo grasped his bow and arrows more firmly and began to follow. Elephant trumpeted to the sky for help. But Thunder growled back, "It is useless to ask for help now. I warned you and you did nothing. You can't tell what

a man is thinking by what he *says*, you can only tell by what he *does*. It is too late." From that time to this Dorobo has always hunted Elephant, and so have all men that have come after him.

As for Elephant, he has never again laughed at Dorobo, and has kept as far away from him as he can.

A GUIDE TO QUESTION TYPES

Below are different types of questions you might ask while reading. Notice that it isn't always important (or even possible) to answer all questions right away. The questions below are about "Thank You, M'am" (pp. 13–21).

Factual questions are about the story and have one correct answer that you can find by looking back at the story.	Why does Roger fall on the sidewalk? (Answer: He loses his balance when he tries to snatch Mrs. Jones's purse.) What does Mrs. Jones do for a living? (Answer: She works in a hotel beauty shop.)
Vocabulary questions are about words or phrases in the story. They can be answered with the glossary (pp. 139–159), a dictionary, or *context clues*—parts of the story near the word that give hints about its meaning.	Is a "pocketbook" the same as a purse? What does "half nelson" mean? (Practice finding context clues on pages 15–16 to figure out the meaning of this phrase.)
Background questions are often about a story's location, time period, or culture. You can answer them with information from a source like the Internet or an encyclopedia.	How long ago is this story set, if Roger can buy a new pair of shoes for ten dollars? What kind of house is a rooming house?

Speculative questions ask about events or details that are not covered in the story. You must guess at or invent your answers.

> Will Roger buy blue suede shoes with the money Mrs. Jones gives him?
>
> What are the things Mrs. Jones did that she won't tell Roger about?

Evaluative questions ask for your personal opinion about something in the story, like whether a character does the right thing. These questions have more than one good answer. Support for these answers comes from your beliefs and experiences as well as the story.

> Was Mrs. Jones right to give Roger the money after he tried to steal from her?
>
> Would you have tried to run away from Mrs. Jones?

Interpretive questions ask about the deep meaning of the story and are the focus of a Shared Inquiry discussion. They have more than one good answer. Support for these answers comes only from evidence in the story.

> Why does Mrs. Jones call Roger "son"?
>
> Why can't Roger say "thank you" to Mrs. Jones at the end of the story?

GLOSSARY

In this glossary, you'll find definitions for words that you may not know but that are in the stories you've read. You'll find the meaning of each word as it is used in the story. The word may have other meanings as well, which you can find in a dictionary if you're interested. If you don't find a word here that you are wondering about, go to your dictionary for help.

absorbing: Something is **absorbing** if it captures all your attention. *The movie was so **absorbing** that no one heard the doorbell ring.*

accustomed: If you are **accustomed** to something, you are used to it. *If you are on a sports team, you grow **accustomed** to having after-school practice every week.*

admonishingly: If you speak to someone **admonishingly,** you scold that person in a kind but serious way. *"Don't wander off again—I was so worried," the girl's mother said **admonishingly**.*

anoraks: Heavy hooded jackets that are usually waterproof.

arrogant: If you are **arrogant** you act like a snob and think you are better than others. *The arrogant girl in my class thinks she is smarter than all of us.*

astonishment: Surprise, shock, or amazement because something is very unusual or unexpected. *You might feel astonishment if your mother serves you ice cream for breakfast.*

au revoir: French for "goodbye."

barren: Something is **barren** when it is bare or has nothing growing in it. *After I took down all my pictures, the walls of my room were barren.*

beaters: In a hunt, **beaters** are the people who hit the bushes so that the animals or birds will come out into the open.

blacksmith: A **blacksmith** is a person who makes horseshoes and other things out of iron.

blue suede shoes: A style of fancy shoes that were popular with teenagers in the 1950s.

blundering: Clumsy. *The blundering child knocked over a tower of blocks as he walked across the room.*

boomerangs: When an action or an object **boomerangs**, it returns to where it came from, sometimes with unplanned or negative results. *When I throw the ball, it boomerangs off a tree and heads back toward me, hitting me in the arm.*

borscht: A soup made with beets and other vegetables.

brim: The top edge of a container. *If you have a glass that is filled to the **brim**, you should carry it very carefully so it won't spill.*

brittle: Something **brittle** can break or snap easily or seems as though it can. *The grass looked **brittle** with its coat of winter frost.*

broach: To bring up an idea or a subject in a conversation because you want to talk about it. *You might not want to **broach** the idea of going to the movies if your parents are tired.*

bustle: When you **bustle**, you rush around or move with a lot of energy. *Before a party, everyone will **bustle** around the house, cleaning and cooking.*

captive: Someone or something that is held prisoner or kept under the control of another. *A criminal is a **captive** in his jail cell.*

caressed: If you **caress** something, you touch or stroke it gently, in a loving way. *The father **caressed** his baby's cheek with his fingertips.*

caulking: A material you put into holes or cracks to keep out water or air. *He patched the leaking roof with **caulking**.*

ceased: Something has **ceased** if it has stopped or come to an end. *The music suddenly **ceased** and the room was silent.*

141

chided: To **chide** is to speak in a way that shows you are disappointed in someone. *My teacher **chided** me for forgetting my homework again.*

clambered: To **clamber** is to climb with difficulty, often using both your hands and feet. *The children **clambered** up the steep, muddy hill.*

clamped: Joined together tightly. *I kept my hands **clamped** together so that the firefly I was holding would not escape.*

cleats: Special shoes with rubber or metal bumps on the bottom, worn by athletes to keep them from slipping. *The football players wore **cleats** to help them run in the rain.*

commitment: A **commitment** is a promise to carry out an action. *I can't go to the baseball game because I made a **commitment** to go to a play the same day.*

concealed: To **conceal** something is to hide it, so that others cannot find it. *The dog searched the yard for the bone, but a pile of dirt **concealed** it from him.*

condescending: Someone who is **condescending** acts as if she is better than other people and talks down to them. *The king was very **condescending** to his servants, speaking to them as if they were children.*

confide: When you **confide** in people, you tell them things that you usually keep private. *I will **confide** in my best friend and tell her that I am afraid of the dark.*

conscience: Your **conscience** is the feeling you have about what is right and what is wrong. *She was going to pretend to be sick so she could stay home from school, but her* **conscience** *wouldn't let her tell a lie.* When you do something **in good conscience**, you do it fairly or truthfully. *I found a wallet on the street, but I returned it to its owner* **in good conscience.**

considerable: Fairly large in size or amount. *There was a* **considerable** *crowd of people at the concert, so they had to add extra seats.*

continually: Something that happens **continually** happens again and again or without stopping. *It snows* **continually** *in Alaska.*

cress: A plant with leaves that can be eaten in salads; it often has a strong peppery taste.

crinkled: Something is **crinkled** if it has lots of lines or wrinkles. *The paper was* **crinkled** *from being folded so many times.*

cunning: Someone who is **cunning** is good at tricking or fooling people. *The* **cunning** *salesman is often able to sell things for twice as much as they are worth.*

defiantly: When you do something **defiantly**, you boldly refuse to follow orders or rules. *The student behaved* **defiantly** *when he wouldn't line up with the other children.*

definite: Certain and without doubt. *A multiple-choice test question has one* ***definite*** *correct answer.* Something **definite** can also be something that is exact, with clear limits or borders. *We set a* ***definite*** *time to meet, but my friend was still late.*

dignified: Calm, controlled, and confident. *He accepted his award at the school ceremony in a* ***dignified*** *way.*

disdain: When you show **disdain**, you act as if someone is not worthy of your respect or attention. *She rolled her eyes in* ***disdain*** *at the boy's rude behavior.*

disgraced: You are **disgraced** if you do something that makes people lose respect for you or makes you feel shame. *The students were* ***disgraced*** *when the teacher caught them cheating on a test.*

disgruntled: Someone who is **disgruntled** is unhappy or unsatisfied—and lets others know. *The students were* ***disgruntled*** *when the cafeteria stopped making its best dish.*

disgusted: If you are **disgusted**, you find something very unpleasant or you have a strong feeling of dislike. *We were* ***disgusted*** *by the overflowing garbage cans in the park.*

dubiously: Showing doubt. *"You're really going to read that whole book in one night?" my mother asked me* ***dubiously***.

dungeon: A dark prison that is often built underground. *The king locked the worst criminals in the **dungeon** underneath the castle.*

embedding: Surrounding firmly and tightly. *Fossils are made when the sand or dirt **embedding** small creatures and plants hardens to stone over thousands of years.*

etched: Something **etched** is cut into the surface of something (like wood, glass, or other material). *A fancy design was **etched** into the wood using a sharp tool.*

exception: A person or thing that is different or left out. *Everyone in my family has brown eyes, but my little brother is the **exception** because he has blue eyes.*

exposed: When something is **exposed**, it is left uncovered or out in the open. *When we got out of the car, we were **exposed** to the pouring rain.*

foreboding: A feeling that something bad is about to happen. *You might watch a very scary movie with **foreboding**.*

frail: Weak. *After his long illness, the boy was **frail** and got tired easily.*

frantic: If you are **frantic**, you are stirred up by worry or fear. *The little girl was **frantic** when she thought her mother left the store without her.*

generous: Something **generous** is larger or better than expected. *My mother gave me such a **generous** piece of apple pie I couldn't finish it all.* **Generous** also means unselfish and happy to share things. *The **generous** boy let everyone in his class have a piece of his candy.*

gesture: A **gesture** is a movement of the head or body to help show feeling. *When you are excited, you might **gesture** with your hands while you talk.* A **gesture** is also something that a person says or does just for show, knowing that it won't have an effect on anything. *My father said he would punish me, but I could tell it was just a **gesture** because he wasn't really angry.*

gleaner: Someone who picks up the grain left behind in a field after crops have been gathered.

grumbling: Making a low, deep, rolling sound. *My stomach was **grumbling** because I was so hungry.* **Grumbling** also means complaining in a low, grouchy voice. *My brother is always **grumbling** about having to take out the trash.*

half nelson: A kind of wrestling hold.

hauled: To **haul** something means to pull or drag it with force. *The men **hauled** the heavy tree branches away by tying ropes to them and pulling them behind a truck.*

hawking: Using trained hawks for hunting.

hillock: A small hill.

hospitable: Someone who is **hospitable** treats visitors or guests in a friendly and welcoming way. *The server at our favorite restaurant is very **hospitable** and always greets us with a big smile.*

hue and cry: A noisy public demand or protest.

icebox: Another name for a refrigerator. An **icebox** is also a cabinet that holds a large block of ice to keep food cold.

idling: If you are **idling**, you passing the time without doing any work. *The children spent their time **idling** in front of the television instead of doing their school project.*

ignorant: You are **ignorant** if you have very little knowledge or education about something. *He said some **ignorant** things in class because he hadn't read the book we were talking about.*

imitation: If you do an **imitation** of someone, you copy how they act or sound. *My friend did a perfect **imitation** of our teacher, walking and talking exactly like him.*

implored: To **implore** is to beg or ask for something you want badly. *The prisoner **implored** the judge to let him go free.*

incompetent: An **incompetent** person doesn't know how to do something or cannot do it well. *The piano player was so* ***incompetent*** *that we couldn't tell what she was trying to play.*

joints: A **joint** is a place where two or more parts of something come together. *In your body, the meeting of your leg and thigh bones are your knee* ***joints****. An umbrella folds easily because of the* ***joints*** *in its metal structure.*

kimchi: A traditional Korean dish made of vegetables such as cabbage, radish, and cucumber. ***Kimchi*** *has a very strong taste from being salted, spiced, and* fermented *(a slow, natural chemical process that breaks down sugar).*

kitchenette: A small kitchen area.

larder: A small room or closet where food is stored. *The* ***larder*** *was empty, so I was not able to make myself anything to eat.*

latching: If you **latch** on to something, you grab onto it and hold it tightly. *The puppy keeps* ***latching*** *on to the rope with its teeth and pulling hard.*

lateral: On the side or to the side. *Most crabs walk using a* ***lateral*** *motion instead of moving forward.*

lattice: A **lattice** is formed when strips of something (like metal or wood) are laid across each other to make a crisscross pattern.

lavish: Something **lavish** is grand and expensive; more so than is needed. *She threw a lavish party with fancy food and a live band.*

lee: The sheltered side of something. *You might climb the lee of a hill to avoid the strong wind blowing against the other side.*

lichen: A life form made up of fungus and algae growing together. *Lichen looks a lot like moss and most often grows on rocks and trees.*

lingered: If you **linger** somewhere, you are slow to leave because you do not want to go. *We lingered at the party for so long that our hosts fell asleep!*

loyalty: Strong and faithful support for someone or something. *The knight showed loyalty by fighting for his king in many battles.*

mesh: Threads or wires joined loosely together to form a net. *The screen in a screen door is made of wire mesh.*

miser: A **miser** is a person who does not want to spend or share any money. *My dad is such a miser that he saves wrapping paper from our holiday gifts and uses it for our birthday presents.*

mistrusted: If you **mistrust** someone, you do not trust that person. *I have mistrusted my friend ever since I found out that she was talking behind my back.*

mortar, pestle: A **mortar** is a deep, heavy bowl, and a **pestle** is a small rounded tool. *A **mortar** and **pestle** can be used to crush spices into powder or paste.*

mussels: A **mussel** is a type of shellfish. ***Mussels** have narrow, blue-black shells.*

muted: A **muted** sound is quiet and unclear because something is blocking or softening it. *We heard **muted** laughter from behind the closed door.*

nondescript: If something is **nondescript**, it doesn't have many things about it that makes it easy to remember or describe. *One pebble on a beach would be **nondescript** unless it was a different color or shape than the rest.*

nuzzled: To **nuzzle** is to rub or touch something gently with the nose. *My dog **nuzzled** my hand happily when I got home from school.*

obedience: When you show **obedience**, you do what you are asked or told. *The captain of the ship expected **obedience** from his crew whenever he gave an order.*

occasionally: When something is **occasional**, it happens sometimes but not often. *My cousins don't live close to us, but they visit **occasionally**.*

overcame: If you **overcome** something, you get control of it or deal with it. *The girl **overcame** her shyness and gave a speech in front of her class.*

parish: A **parish** is an area that has its own church and its own priest or minister.

Passover: A Jewish holiday lasting eight days in the spring to remember the escape of the Jews from slavery in Egypt.

peasants: In the past, a **peasant** was a person who worked on or owned a small farm. *Many **peasants** farmed land in Europe and parts of Asia.*

pining: When you are **pining**, you feel unhappy because you miss something or want something you cannot have. *You might spend the winter **pining** for the days when it was sunny and warm outside.*

plaited: Braided.

poised: Calm and confident. *A **poised** person might not get worried or upset very easily.*

pondered: To **ponder** is to think carefully about something. *The girl **pondered** whether she really wanted to go to a party where she wouldn't know anyone.*

ponderously: Done in a heavy and clumsy way. *If you had a broken leg, you might walk **ponderously** on your crutches.*

pounces: To **pounce** is to leap or drop down suddenly and grab something. *My cat stares at the ball of string before she **pounces** on it.*

pound boat: A fishing boat with a flat bottom and straight sides. People from Sand Island will tell you "**pound boat**" is pronounced "pond boat."

precisely: Exactly. *My grandmother always gives me **precisely** what I want for my birthday because she knows me so well.*

presentable: When you make something **presentable**, you make it fit to be seen by others. *I need to change out of my dirty clothes so that I look more **presentable**.*

profit: A gain or a benefit from doing something. *We spent $5 to make lemonade and we made $10 selling it, so we made a **profit** of $5.*

pullets: Young hens.

rabbi: A leader and teacher of the Jewish religion.

ranker: Something **rank** is growing very thickly. *Plants and grasses are **ranker** in a wet area than in a dry one.* **Rank** also means to have a strong or rotten smell. *Meat that isn't kept in a refrigerator will grow **ranker** over time.*

refreshed: If you are **refreshed**, you have new energy. *If you are tired, you might be **refreshed** by a short nap.* To be **refreshed** also means to be made cool, damp, or clean. *A dip in the pool made the hot, sweaty child feel **refreshed**.*

reproached: When you **reproach** someone, you blame him or tell him you are not happy with his behavior. *My mother reproached me for walking through the house with muddy shoes.*

resolute: Firm and steady in purpose. *The confident woman gave a speech in a loud, resolute voice.*

retorted: When you **retort**, you answer quickly and sharply. *When the boy complained about his burnt toast, his sister retorted that he should make his own.*

revealing: To **reveal** something is to show it or bring it into view. *The curtains on the stage lifted, revealing the actors in the play.*

roomers: People who rent rooms in another person's house or building.

roost: To rest or sleep in a place where a bird might sleep. *Birds often roost in nests, birdhouses, and coops.*

Sabbath: The day of the week used for worship. *For Jewish people, the Sabbath begins at sundown on Friday and ends at sundown on Saturday.*

sarcastic: A **sarcastic** person uses mean or bitter words that are meant to make fun of or hurt someone. *He dislikes the teacher, so he always gives sarcastic answers to her questions.*

scoured: To **scour** something is to clear it out or clean it with force. *The ocean waves **scoured** the beach until no shells or rocks were left.* To **scour** also means to move through or over an area quickly and completely. *I **scoured** my bedroom looking for my lost library book.*

scrabbled: To **scrabble** is to scrape quickly or wildly at something with your hands. *The boy **scrabbled** in the dirt to find the coins that he dropped.*

scrawny: Skinny and bony. *Turkeys and chickens have **scrawny** legs.*

scrimmage: A practice game, usually between members of the same sports team.

scythe: A tool that has a curved blade and a long handle, used for cutting grass or crops.

sheen: A shine on the surface of something. *If you polish a piece of wooden furniture with oil, it will have a nice **sheen**.*

shod: A horse is **shod** when it has horseshoes on its hooves.

shrewd: Clever or tricky. *My sister is good at board games, so I have to be quite **shrewd** to beat her.*

sincere: When you act **sincere**, you act in an honest and true way, without pretending. *When she saw that she had hurt her friend's feelings, she gave a **sincere** apology.*

slung: When something is **slung**, it is placed to hang loosely or swing freely. *The student **slung** his backpack onto his back, almost hitting his friend.*

snatch: To **snatch** something is to quickly grab something that belongs to someone else. *The police were looking for the person who **snatched** the money from the shop's counter.*

sneered: To **sneer** is to make a face or speak in a way that shows you dislike something very much or are making fun of it. *The bully **sneered** at my brother and called him rude names.*

snug: When you say that a boat is **snug**, you mean that it is fit to sail. *The boat will be **snug** once the sails are mended.*

soothed: To **soothe** is to calm someone down or make them feel better. *When the baby cries, he can usually be **soothed** by being rocked gently.*

speculatively: If you say or do something **speculatively**, you do it in a way that shows you are curious about it or testing it out. *I **speculatively** touched the bottom of the lake with my toes to see if it was sandy or rocky.*

sprinting: When you **sprint**, you run very fast for a short distance. *You have to be good at **sprinting** to win a fifty-yard dash.*

square: In the story, to **square** is to make things even or right with someone. *I will square my friend by paying back the money she lent me.*

squire: An English country gentleman.

stammered: When you **stammer**, you speak in an unsure way, stopping often and repeating sounds or words without meaning to. *The nervous girl stammered whenever she had to speak in front of the class.*

stem to stern: From the front end to the back end of a ship.

stinginess: Not wanting to spend money or share things with others, even when you have plenty. *If your brother won't give you any of his candy, you might accuse him of stinginess.*

stocky: Having a solid, heavy body. *Weightlifters and professional football players are often stocky.*

stone drag: A **stone drag** (also called a *stoneboat*) is a flat sled that can move heavy objects, such as stones.

stooped: If you are **stooped**, your head and shoulders are bent forward and down. *When you are trying to find something you dropped on the ground, you might walk in a stooped way.*

subsides: When something **subsides,** it comes down to a normal or less active level. *Once the noise subsides, we will be able to hear ourselves talk.*

substance: A **substance** is the material something is made of or a material of a certain kind. *A cloud is a soft **substance**, while a rock is a hard **substance**.*

supremely: Very greatly or highly. *The Grand Canyon is **supremely** deep and wide.*

surged: To **surge** is to rush forward like a wave. *When the bell rang for recess, the class **surged** onto the playground.*

suspicious: When you are **suspicious**, you think something or someone might be bad or wrong, but you don't have solid proof. *When I asked my sister where my candy bar was, her guilty look made me **suspicious** that she had taken it.*

tempted: When you're **tempted** by something, you want to do or to have it very much, even if it's wrong or foolish. *He was **tempted** to open the gift he found in the closet, even though his birthday was still a week away.*

tentatively: To do something **tentatively** is to do it in an unsure way. *If you think you know the answer to a question but you aren't sure, you might raise your hand **tentatively**.*

tethering: To **tether** something is to tie it to something else to keep it in place. *The woman climbed out of her boat after **tethering** it to the dock so it wouldn't float away.*

timidly: If you do something **timidly**, you do it in a shy and easily frightened way. *My baby sister hides behind me timidly when she meets strangers.*

topple: When something **topples**, it wobbles and then falls over. *The tall stack of books began to topple off the desk.*

trampled: To **trample** something is to crush or ruin it by walking heavily on it. *The flowerbeds were flattened when the dogs trampled them.*

transaction: A deal or trade. *Whenever you buy anything at a store, you are part of a transaction.*

translate: To **translate** is to change written or spoken words from one language to another. *My father only understands Spanish, so I have to translate when someone speaks English to him.*

upholstery: The stuffing, springs, cushions, and cloth coverings used to make furniture like chairs and couches.

vague: Not clear or certain. *You can only see vague shapes of things when it's foggy outside.*

varsity: A **varsity** team is the top team that a school sends to a competition. *Only the best players make the varsity volleyball team.*

vegetation: The different kinds of plants that grow in a certain area. *The **vegetation** in a jungle looks very different from the **vegetation** in a desert.*

venturing: To **venture** is to go ahead and do something dangerous or daring even though it is a risk. *You could get hurt **venturing** across a busy street during rush hour.*

wheel away: To turn around quickly and go.

whorled: Something that is **whorled** has a spiral pattern, curving around and outward from a center point. *Snail shells, spiral staircases, and tornadoes are all **whorled**.*

ACKNOWLEDGMENTS

All possible care has been taken to trace ownership and secure permission for each selection in this series. The Great Books Foundation wishes to thank the following authors, publishers, and representatives for permission to reproduce copyrighted material:

Thank You, M'am, from SHORT STORIES, by Langston Hughes. Copyright © 1996 by Ramona Bass and Arnold Rampersad. Reproduced by permission of Hill and Wang, a division of Farrar, Straus and Giroux, LLC.

CROW CALL, by Lois Lowry. Copyright © 2009 by Lois Lowry. Reproduced by permission of Scholastic Inc.

Fresh, from WHAT THE NEIGHBOURS DID AND OTHER STORIES, by Philippa Pearce. Copyright © 1959 by Philippa Pearce. Reproduced by permission of Laura Cecil Literary Agency on behalf of the author.

Shrewd Todie and Lyzer the Miser, from WHEN SHLEMIEL WENT TO WARSAW AND OTHER STORIES, by Isaac Bashevis Singer. Translation copyright © 1968 by Isaac Bashevis Singer and Elizabeth Shub. Reproduced by permission of Farrar Straus and Giroux, LLC.

ON SAND ISLAND, by Jacqueline Briggs Martin. Copyright © 2003 by Jacqueline Briggs Martin. Reproduced by permission of Houghton Mifflin Harcourt Publishing Company.

THE GREEN MAN, by Gail E. Haley. Copyright © 1979 by Gail E. Haley. Reproduced by permission of the author.

Song of Hope, by Peggy Duffy, from LAY-UPS AND LONG SHOTS. Copyright © 2008 by Peggy Duffy. Published by Darby Creek Publishing. Reproduced by permission of the author.

Jean Labadie's Big Black Dog, from THE TALKING CAT AND OTHER STORIES OF FRENCH CANADA, by Natalie Savage Carlson. Copyright © 1952 by Natalie Savage Carlson. Reproduced by permission of HarperCollins Publishers.

Thunder, Elephant, and Dorobo, from TALES TOLD NEAR A CROCODILE, by Humphrey Harman. Copyright © 1962 by Humphrey Harman. Reproduced by permission of the estate of the author.

ILLUSTRATION CREDITS

Rich Lo prepared the illustrations for *Thank You M'am.*

Bagram Ibatoulline's illustrations for *Crow Call* are from CROW CALL. Illustrations copyright © 2009 by Bagram Ibatoulline. Reproduced by permission of Scholastic Inc.

Emily McCully prepared the illustrations for *Fresh.*

Rosalind Kaye prepared the illustrations for *Shrewd Todie and Lyzer the Miser.*

David A. Johnson's illustrations for *On Sand Island* are from ON SAND ISLAND. Illustrations copyright © 2003 by David A. Johnson. Reproduced by permission of Houghton Mifflin Harcourt Publishing Company.

Brock Cole prepared the illustrations for *The Green Man.*

Terry Julien prepared the illustrations for *Song of Hope.*

Diane Cole prepared the illustrations for *Jean Labadie's Big Black Dog.*

Kathleen A. Wilson prepared the illustrations for *Thunder, Elephant, and Dorobo.*

Cover art by Helen Cann.

Design by THINK Book Works.